Transforming Pakistan
Ways out of instability

Hilary Synnott

Transforming Pakistan
Ways out of instability

Hilary Synnott

IISS The International Institute for Strategic Studies

The International Institute for Strategic Studies

Arundel House | 13–15 Arundel Street | Temple Place | London | WC2R 3DX | UK

First published August 2009 by **Routledge**
4 Park Square, Milton Park, Abingdon, Oxon, OX14 4RN

for **The International Institute for Strategic Studies**
Arundel House, 13–15 Arundel Street, Temple Place, London, WC2R 3DX, UK
www.iiss.org

Simultaneously published in the USA and Canada by **Routledge**
270 Madison Ave., New York, NY 10016

Routledge is an imprint of Taylor & Francis, an Informa Business

© 2009 The International Institute for Strategic Studies

DIRECTOR-GENERAL AND CHIEF EXECUTIVE John Chipman
EDITOR Tim Huxley
MANAGER FOR EDITORIAL SERVICES Ayse Abdullah
ASSISTANT EDITOR Katharine Fletcher
COVER/PRODUCTION John Buck

The International Institute for Strategic Studies is an independent centre for research, information and debate on the problems of conflict, however caused, that have, or potentially have, an important military content. The Council and Staff of the Institute are international and its membership is drawn from almost 100 countries. The Institute is independent and it alone decides what activities to conduct. It owes no allegiance to any government, any group of governments or any political or other organisation. The IISS stresses rigorous research with a forward-looking policy orientation and places particular emphasis on bringing new perspectives to the strategic debate.

The Institute's publications are designed to meet the needs of a wider audience than its own membership and are available on subscription, by mail order and in good book-shops. Further details at www.iiss.org.

Printed and bound in Great Britain by Bell & Bain Ltd, Thornliebank, Glasgow

British Library Cataloguing in Publication Data
A catalogue record for this book is available from the British Library

Library of Congress Cataloging in Publication Data

ISBN 978-0-41556-260-7
ISSN 0567-932X

ADELPHI 406

Contents

Pakistan

Pakistan and its neighbours

NWFP, the FATA and the Northern Areas

Kashmir

About 200 miles southwest of the city of Quetta in the desert province of Baluchistan, close to Pakistan's border with Afghanistan and Iran, is a small airfield at a place called Shamsi. For many years the airfield was used by wealthy sheikhs from the Gulf and Saudi Arabia to conduct falconry expeditions to hunt the Houbara bustard, a harmless desert bird that features on international lists of endangered species. The sheikhs paid handsome sums to the Pakistani authorities for the privilege of endangering it further although, like so many of Pakistan's financial transactions at that time, details were difficult to find in the annual budget.

After September 2001, when Pakistan had been declared an ally of the US in a collective effort to combat terrorism, Arab revenue for the use of the airfield was replaced by US funding to compensate Pakistan for its military support. In early 2009, *The Times* reported that, according to satellite imagery, Shamsi was the launch pad for attacks by US *Predator* drones on Pakistan's Federally Administered Tribal Areas (FATA).[1] A few months earlier, the Pakistani president, prime minister and parliament had roundly condemned US drone attacks as violations

of Pakistani sovereignty, calling for them to be halted immediately. The Pakistani government denied that any US forces
were based in Pakistan.

Whatever the truth about the use of Shamsi, there was no
doubt that, having authorised another drone strike to take place
just three days after his inauguration, President Barack Obama
was determined that these attacks should continue.[2] Some two
months later, launching a new US strategy for Afghanistan and
Pakistan, Obama urged Congress to approve a sizeable package
of new, non-military aid that would go some way towards
balancing the approximately $10 billion in overt funding that
the US had supplied Pakistan for primarily military purposes
over the previous seven years.

These brief facts give an indication of the profound difficulties in forging relations with Pakistan. Although Pakistan is an
ally, the US has felt it necessary to launch attacks in its sovereign
territory, at least one of which, in September 2008, involved
the use of ground forces. The US welcomed Pakistan's elections in February 2008 as a return to democracy, but continued
the attacks despite condemnation from Pakistan's democratic
institutions. Meanwhile, a dramatic surge of violent extremism
from within Pakistan, distinct from and largely independent
of al-Qaeda, threatened the state itself. And even moderate
Pakistanis declare that their country is 'fighting Washington's
war'.

On the face of it, therefore, US strategy has involved contra-
dictions that are not only intellectually uncomfortable, but
which may have been positively counterproductive.

There can be no doubt that the widespread violence within
the country makes it 'Pakistan's war' as well. But the growth of
this violence and the formerly rare practice of suicide bombing
also suggests that part of the problem lies in the perception,
and the reality, of successive Pakistani governments' support

for US military operations. The army, which has tradition-ally assumed the role of 'guardian of the nation', as witnessed most recently in General Pervez Musharraf's military coup ten years ago, has been conducting a violent campaign against its countrymen for more than five years. It claims in the process to have suffered more losses and casualties than all the Coalition forces in Afghanistan combined.[3] The failure of its repeated efforts to quash outbursts of violence in the tribal regions, and the collapse of several peace agreements, have been a severe humiliation for Pakistan's military. The sustainability of its renewed efforts to pacify Swat and Waziristan that began in mid 2009 will thus be an important test of its effectiveness.

At the same time, Pakistan has experienced an acute economic crisis, so much so that President Asif Ali Zardari was forced in 2008 to renege on a post-inaugural pledge and seek financial support from the International Monetary Fund (IMF). The combined effects of the depreciation of Pakistan's currency and the country's dependence on oil and food imports hit ordi-nary people hard. In 2009, prospects for the large proportion of the population who live at or below the poverty line looked bleaker than at any time since the country split in two after the India–Pakistan War of 1971.

Nor have the democratic elections of early 2008 and the subsequent election of Zardari to the presidency facilitated the management of Pakistan's many challenges, despite his clear majority in the national and provincial assemblies. On the contrary, the president's deep unpopularity within the country as a whole extended to his own party after he replaced Benazir Bhutto's key advisers with his own largely unknown team. His main political rival Nawaz Sharif, furious over Zardari's refusal to honour, among others, his pledges to undo the constitutional changes instituted by Musharraf, proved unwilling to tackle Pakistan's difficulties in coalition with the president's party, even when the country was experiencing multiple crises, and seemed determined instead to bring the new president down.

What, amid all the uncertainty, denials and obfuscations, has really been happening in Pakistan? How did it come to this? Has the country become ungovernable, a failed state? Do the challenges to the state's authority emanating from the tribal areas suggest a descent into violent anarchy that will make the country a refuge and breeding ground for the very forces that the US-led Coalition has been combating in the region since 2001?

This book does not presume to give definitive answers to each of these questions. It seeks, rather, to provide material with which to inform judgements, both about the significance of events that have occurred and that might occur in future, and about policies that might be pursued by countries that wish Pakistan and its people well.

Pakistan's present is inextricably linked to its history, relatively brief as it is. The country's relationship with democracy has been deformed by repeated interventions in national politics by the army which, while being presented as attempts to forestall disaster, have strengthened the army's own institutional position and increased its influence in non-military affairs. The flawed governance of successive civilian administrations has had its own undermining effects, as have some of the actions of outsiders in Pakistan and its region. Current problems have roots too in the difficulties Pakistan has had in forging a common national identity among diverse ethnic and linguistic groups, notably in the tribal regions.

This book surveys Pakistan's troubled recent history and examines the implications of its fraught internal dynamics for the wider world. It seems clear that the challenges that face Pakistan could, if left unchecked, pose severe risks to the interests of the West and others. Managing and reducing these risks will require far more effort, investment and sensitivity than has hitherto been shown, either by Pakistan's governments or by the country's friends and allies. Events since the beginning of the Afghanistan campaign in 2001 and, especially, since Pakistan's military began operations in the tribal areas in 2004 have shown – if it were not already obvious – that the challenges cannot by dealt with by military means alone and, indeed, that military approaches have too often made matters worse. The objective can no longer be limited to simple containment or temporary stabilisation.

The book argues that Pakistan's structural and historical weaknesses are such that nothing short of a transformation of the country's body politic and institutions will be necessary. The need for this transformation, which can only be brought about by Pakistan itself, is increasingly recognised within the country. Such change ought to be achievable: the depredations of the past decades have not entirely eroded the functional elements of the country's infrastructure and habits – Pakistan is not yet a failed state. But a transformation towards durable stability will take time and much care to achieve. And it will require a great deal of external help, of a kind that takes account of the country's cultural and economic diversity and the legitimate interests of its many ethnic groupings. Above all, this external help must not be imposed upon the Pakistani people against their will, and it must focus at least as much on non-military as on military matters.

In a country with great needs but limited absorptive capacity, it would be foolish to expect rapid results or, indeed, to expect changes to mirror the ideals and ideologies of outsiders. But progress will be immeasurably aided to the extent that the actions of outsiders are guided less by their own short-term interests than by consideration for the long-term good of all involved. The transformation of Pakistan requires a transformation of Pakistanis' attitudes towards those who call themselves friends, from suspicion towards trust. If this were to come about, much else could follow.

CHAPTER ONE

The Nature of Pakistan

The difficulties of nation-building

At the end of the British-dominated colonial era in the sub-continent, India achieved its long-sought objective of independence in 1947. But the break with Britain was a secondary objective for Pakistan, whose primary goal was to provide a Muslim homeland, separate from the new India dominated by Hindus, for those Muslims on the subcontinent who wished to live there. The new country's *Qaid-e-Azam*, or Great Leader, Mohammad Ali Jinnah, aimed to establish a liberal Muslim democracy. But the ensuing arrangement proved to be both bloody and inherently unstable. Vivid memories remain, in both India and Pakistan, of the mass movement of people, family separations and violence that caused at least half a million, and possibly twice as many, deaths. The Kashmir dispute, over which there was a war immediately following the birth of the two new countries and several more conflicts subsequently, is still described by Pakistan as 'the unfinished business of Partition' more than 60 years after that event.

From the outset, the Pakistani people have had difficulty subsuming their particular ethnic customs and identities into a single national narrative. Unfavourable comparisons are often made with India in this regard. But the differences between the beginnings of the two nations are often overlooked. At Partition, India inherited the state governance structure created by the British, including the civil service, the executive branch and the parliamentary system. India also possessed a highly developed historical sense of national identity, linked to ancient civilisations. But Pakistan had to create, or at least adapt, all these crucial elements of nationhood for itself. It was only in 1940 that the goal of independent statehood for the Muslim-majority areas was formally adopted by the Muslim League, the main Muslim political movement in India, just seven years before this goal was achieved. By contrast, the Indian National Congress had committed itself to national unity and independence in 1921, and this aim was thus familiar to an entire generation of Indians before it was realised.[1] In contrast with nearly 17 years of the prime ministership of Jawaharlal Nehru in India, Pakistan lacked durable leadership: Jinnah died in September 1948; the country's first prime minister, Liaquat Ali Khan, was assassinated in October 1951. Pakistan's army, which emerged out of the army that existed under the British, was the country's most firmly established institution, and its most self-confident. Witnessing the weaknesses of the civilian political establishment, it intervened frequently and vigorously in national politics to become, in effect, Pakistan's oldest and most powerful political party. The Indian armed forces, on the other hand, have always been subject to elected politicians.

It is perhaps unsurprising that religion, the stated basis for Pakistan's separation from India, was on its own not enough to create a durable national identity. This is particularly so when one considers the diversity of the peoples and religious and customary practices in what is now the second-largest Muslim nation in the world.[2] While Pakistan is the only country to have been created on the basis of a common Muslim identity, Pakistani Muslims have in practice been deeply divided about the nature and practice of their faith. Some 75% of Pakistanis describe themselves as Sunni Muslims, of whom the great majority are of the Hanafi sect, while about 20% of the population is Shia. The country has a history of violence between Sunni and Shia. Many Pakistanis also remain strongly influenced by the Sufi tradition, which is unrelated to the Sunni/Shia split.

Among Hanafi Sunni there are deep differences over observance and doctrine, of which the most significant are those between the Barelvis and the Deobandis. The Barelvis, whose movement originated in the town of Bareilly in northern India in the late nineteenth century, form the majority of Pakistani Sunnis, and have a comparatively moderate and tolerant interpretation of Islam. Although the movement's founder opposed the devotional practices of Sufism, including the use of poetry, literature, mysticism, music and dance, many Barelvis follow them.

Deobandis, in contrast, have always been more radical and militant. Also founded in India, shortly before the Barelvi movement, unlike that group, the Deobandi movement rejected Jinnah's vision of a liberal democracy, favouring an Islamic state purged of 'un-Islamic practices'. Its literal and austere interpretation of the faith puts a particular emphasis on education. Students from Deobandi madrasas, which account for around 65% of Pakistan's religious schools, swelled the Taliban movement in Afghanistan when it emerged in 1994–96.

Unable to furnish a basis for a common national identity, religion proved insufficient to hold the state together in its original form. At an early stage in Pakistan's history, when the country was made up of modern-day Pakistan (West Pakistan) and the territory that is now Bangladesh (East Pakistan), the Awami League party emerged in East Pakistan seeking greater autonomy for the Bengali population that formed the overwhelming majority in the East. Later, in December 1970, under the leadership of Mujibur Rahman, the party swept the polls in East Pakistan and, despite gaining no seats in West Pakistan, secured enough seats for an absolute majority in the National Assembly. Pakistan's military ruler, General Yahya Khan, and Zulfikar Ali Bhutto, the leader of West Pakistan's largest party (which had gained no seats in the East), refused to accept the outcome of the election. An ensuing civil war between the East and West wings of the country, 1,000 miles apart from each other, escalated into a war with India as well, and finished with the spectacular defeat of Pakistan's army, the secession of East Pakistan and the creation of Bangladesh. The Pakistan founded by Jinnah had lost a sixth of its land mass and more than half its population. It had lasted only 24 years.

Despite this humiliation, which followed defeats in wars with India over Kashmir in 1947–48 and 1965, Pakistan persisted in its attempts to use Islam as a means of nation-building and a way of differentiating itself from India. Frequently, too, religion was used by both the army and elected politicians to promote particular political interests. The army's use of the Kashmir dispute, which has a strong religious element, was an example of this: so long as Kashmir was a cause to fight for and there was an enemy, India, to deal with, the army remained indispensable. National honour and the righteousness of the cause, so the argument went, required that the army be large and well equipped and its personnel well provided for, both in service and retirement. The army's position and Pakistan's Kashmir-related grievances were greatly reinforced by all-too-frequent Indian military heavy-handedness and the use of violence and unjust measures in the region, which included political oppression and the blatant rigging of successive elections in the Indian-administered part of Kashmir over a period of decades.

The various efforts that have been made to cement in place a national consciousness and identity have been quite insufficient for dealing with Pakistan's intra-state tensions. In addition to the diversity of religious practice, the range of long-established cultural, ethnic and linguistic differences within the country, which long predate the state of Pakistan, would have posed formidable challenges for any government. Their associated frictions have proved far too great to be resolved by the flawed politico-military systems that have governed the country over the past six decades.

Attempts at 'Pakistanisation' were reinforced by the nomination of Urdu as a national lingua franca. This was a somewhat artificial device, since Urdu, the spoken form of which has many similarities with Hindi, was not one of Pakistan's indigenous languages, but was imported from India. The plan to bring the disparate cultures of the country closer together through the use of the language has not been entirely successful. Many indigenous languages, such as Sindhi, Pashto, Siraiki and Baluchi, have been used to emphasise ethnic identities – often in order to differentiate speakers from the dominant Punjabi culture – at the expense of national solidarity. It is highly relevant to Pakistan's present-day challenges that Pashto, the dominant language in the northwest of the country and one of the two main languages of Afghanistan, is markedly different from most of the other main languages of the country, coming from the Iranian rather than the Indo-Aryan branch of the Indo-Iranian language family, and is the language least likely to be understood by other Pakistani ethnic groups.

The provinces

The differences between the four provinces that make up most of Pakistan – Punjab, Sindh, the North West Frontier Province (NWFP) and Baluchistan – go beyond language and ethnicity, important though these are. Many of the differences derive from traditions unique to each region.[3] Punjab, described by Jinnah as 'the cornerstone of Pakistan', is home to more than 60% of the country's population, and dominates both the army and the economy. The bulk of Pakistan's industrial infrastructure can be found in Punjab, and the province's fertile land draws off much of the country's scarce water through irrigation. For such reasons it is unloved by many in the other provinces. But even within prosperous Punjab there are great contrasts between rich and poor and between city and country dwellers, as well as linguistic variety.

In rural Sindh, semi-feudal agricultural labourers are almost as dependent on large landowners as their forebears were for centuries. The Indus River, having entered Pakistan as a torrent from Kashmir in the north, flows through Sindh to emerge into the Arabian Sea as a trickle, depleted by irrigation and leakage from poorly maintained canals. The poverty and harsh environment of the Thar Desert in the east of the province contrast with the ostentatiously affluent lifestyle of the many rich traders, entrepreneurs, smugglers and drug barons who have made a home in the provincial capital of Karachi on the coast. After Partition, the city attracted many thousands of *mohajirs*, Muslims who had fled from India, among them the parents of Pervez Musharraf. More recently it has been swelled by hundreds of thousands of Afghan refugees, and has become the largest Pashtun city in the world.

The North West Frontier Province has a mainly Pashtun population including, again, many Afghan refugees. Its principal city, bustling, colourful Peshawar, is a hub on the trade and smuggling route to Afghanistan. Even more than the other provinces, NWFP has maintained a certain political separateness from the federal capital. Some of its districts use tribal and sharia law rather than federal law. Many, if not most, of the men of the tribes carry arms as a matter of personal honour.

The desert province of Baluchistan, which borders Iran and Afghanistan, accounts for 42% of Pakistan's land mass but is home to not much more than 5% of the country's population. Literacy is exceptionally low, especially among women. The water-table in the province has dropped rapidly as a result of the widespread use of tube wells and could even threaten the viability of the provincial capital, Quetta. The increased quantities of livestock sustained by water extracted in this way have decimated the region's sparse vegetation, accelerating desertification. Life has also been made harder by increased pressure on land and resources as a result of large influxes of Pashto-speaking Afghan refugees who fled to the north of the province following war and upheavals in Afghanistan, first during the 1979–89 war, then during the Taliban regime in the 1990s, and again after 2001. Though Baluchistan has substantial mineral, coal and gas deposits, the region's poor population derives little benefit from them, causing great resentment.

Distinct from the four provinces, the other main regions within Pakistan are the semi-autonomous Federally Administered Tribal Areas (FATA), and the Federally Administered Northern Areas and what in Pakistan is known as Azad (Free) Kashmir, both of which formed part of the princely state of Jammu and Kashmir in British India and which are the subject of the dispute with India. Each of these has different arrangements for its administration.

Beyond a resentment of the wealth and political and economic dominance of Punjab, Pakistan's various provinces and regions have little in common. Among the deep-rooted differences and tensions between them are bitter disputes over supply of and access to natural resources such as water and gas, and resentments over the distribution of central funds. Given this, it is perhaps unsurprising that separatist tendencies have emerged frequently over the decades.

The most dramatic separatist moment in Pakistan's history was the secession of the mainly Bengali-speaking East Pakistan in 1971. In Karachi and rural Sindh, violence, variously expressing opposition to Punjabi settlers, friction between indigenous Sindhis and *mohajirs* and Sindhi nationalism, has been endemic since the 1950s. Pashtun separatism and the quest for an independent Pashtun homeland, Pashtunwa, was a powerful force in NWFP from 1947 to 1958; violence erupted again in the province from 1973 to 1977, as it has again since 2001. Protest against central authority in Baluchistan met with particularly bloody responses from the government in 1948, 1958, 1962, 1973–77, and from 2005 to the present day. Some of these movements have had external support, including from the Soviet Union, Afghanistan and, according to the Pakistan authorities, India.[4]

Successive Pakistani leaders have opposed separatism, among them Ayub Khan, Zulfikar Ali Bhutto (who described it as provincialism and small-mindedness) and Musharraf (who vowed to 'crush' dissident Baluchis). But separatist feeling is not easily dismissed, and it remains a threat to Pakistan today, although each case is different in character and significance, and each enjoys a different degree of support.

The army and politics

These existential challenges are reflected in the weaknesses of the country's politics and institutions. Almost every decade of Pakistan's 62-year life has seen a replacement of civilian with military rule. The first military coup, led by General Ayub Khan in 1958, was followed by 11 years with Ayub at the helm, which ended when Yahya Khan, another general, took over in 1969. Yahya Khan led Pakistan for two years, until the disastrous war in 1971. The next military takeover came in 1977, when General Muhammad Zia-ul-Haq deposed and subsequently executed Zulfikar Ali Bhutto. Military rule then lasted until Zia's death in mysterious circumstances in 1988. In 1999, Pervez Musharraf deposed Nawaz Sharif in a third coup, standing down in 2008. In all, Pakistan has been run by generals for more than half of its lifetime.

On taking over, each of the four generals pledged to swiftly restore democracy,[5] while lamenting that the civilian leaders on offer lacked the qualities that would enable them to bring about good governance and democracy themselves. In reality, none of the generals left office voluntarily, although Musharraf decided to resign rather than face almost certain impeachment.

Even when not directly in charge, the army has been politically active behind the scenes. Zulfikar Ali Bhutto and his daughter Benazir each came to office after normal elections following periods of military rule. But Zulfikar Ali Bhutto was deposed by General Zia, and all of Benazir Bhutto's and Nawaz Sharif's terms of office between 1988 and 1999 were brought to premature ends. At least three of Pakistan's prime ministers – Mohammad Khan Junejo in Zia's time, and Mir Zafarullah Khan Jamali and Shaukat Aziz in Musharraf's – were products of elections in which the army had intervened.

Interaction between the military and civilian politicians, therefore, has been, and remains, both active and complex. It merits examination.

The political use of religious parties and militants

In their struggle to exercise, maintain and enhance their power, secular politicians and military leaders alike have made use of the power and influence of religion for their own purposes. One important manifestation of this has been the creation, cooption or support of militant religious groups and their use as proxy or supplementary fighters against real or supposed external threats. In some instances the government has acted overtly, as during the Soviet occupation of Afghanistan. In others, support for militant groups has been covert and officially denied, as in the case of the assisted infiltration of 'freedom fighters' into Indian-administered Kashmir. In electoral politics, religious parties or movements have frequently been wooed in order to secure their support in parliament or to induce them not to oppose some course of action. The plans by Nawaz Sharif, a protégé of General Zia, to introduce sharia law throughout the country in 1999 were an example of this kind of courting. Though electoral support for religious parties has invariably been low – usually of the order of 4–8% – their role in coalition-building tends to give these parties disproportionate influence. On certain occasions, political processes have been manipulated to the advantage of religious parties in order to reduce the influence of one or more of the main traditional political parties. This phenomenon was particularly in evidence during the 2002 general election, when it seemed that the mainstream political parties might defeat the party that had been created to support Musharraf, and the Inter-Services Intelligence Department (ISI) responded by helping an alliance of religious parties to achieve dominance in NWFP, thereby reducing the overall vote for mainstream parties.

The inducements presented to religious and militant groups by those in power have varied according to circumstance. Militants have been supplied with arms and funds, trained, and helped to infiltrate their target areas. Cooperation with a given political party by religious groups has been encouraged by bribery, including the offer of attractive and often lucrative appointments, blackmail, promises of religiously oriented social reforms, a halt to reforms opposed by religious groups, and combinations of these. This expedient approach to religion in politics helps to explain the failure of successive Pakistani governments, even when ostensibly committed to modernisation, moderation and democracy, to rescind regressive legislation such as the notorious Hudood Ordinance, which was instituted in 1979 during Zia's Islamisation process and which has seriously undermined women's rights.[6] All of these techniques for making use of the forces of religion have been employed in recent years, and some continue under the government elected in 2008.

An alliance in Afghanistan

The most significant of these pragmatic relationships between politics and religion was that cultivated by Zia and the CIA and promoted by Western governments and Saudi Arabia during the Soviet occupation of Afghanistan in the 1980s. The damage caused by the mishandling of the consequences of this alliance cannot be overestimated. Its legacy goes a long way towards explaining the nature and extent of militant violence in Pakistan and Afghanistan today.

Although liaison channels between the CIA and its Pakistani counterpart remained open, at the time of the Soviet invasion of Afghanistan in December 1979 – and for a year or so after it – relations between the US and Pakistan could hardly have been worse.[7] US President Jimmy Carter was strongly wedded to the cause of human rights and to nuclear non-proliferation, and was highly critical of Pakistan on these grounds. In April 1979, US economic and military aid to Pakistan had been suspended under the terms of the Symington Amendment. In November 1980, a mob attacked the US embassy in Islamabad, possibly with Zia's connivance, while Pakistani security forces stood by.

When, recognising the changed political imperatives following the Soviet invasion, Carter tried to enlist Zia's support against the Soviets, his offer of $400 million in aid was contemptuously rejected. The Reagan administration that took office soon afterwards raised the offer to $3.2 billion. Thus began an eight-year-long relationship between the US government and a military autocrat that bolstered the unelected institutions of state power, including militant religious forces and Zia himself, to the detriment of democratic influences.[8] Memories and embellished narratives of these times remain fresh in Pakistan and are constant impediments to efforts to improve relations between the US and Pakistan.[9]

The US and its Western allies saw the Soviet invasion in East–West terms. The US was determined that Moscow should not be permitted to get away with such a blatant violation of international law and the integrity of another state, nor to occupy a geographical and political space from which it might gain strategic influence. The Pakistani leadership was more concerned with the implications in relation to India, a long-term ally of the Soviet Union that had refused to condemn the Soviet action and that could be expected to capitalise on a Soviet presence on Pakistan's western flank. Pakistan's interest in Afghanistan was primarily motivated by a strong concern to ensure a compliant, friendly neighbour on its western border in the context of its tensions with India in the east. This concern has informed repeated Pakistani attempts to gain influence with and sometimes control over Afghanistan's rulers.

Much of Pakistan's approach to Afghanistan, in these years and subsequently, also related to the notion of strategic depth. This concept is largely familiar in the context of NATO's Cold War strategy towards the Soviet Union: if faced with advancing Warsaw Pact tanks, the NATO front line could pull back westwards and absorb the initial shock before launching a counter-attack. In the context of possible conflict between Pakistan and India, the idea that Afghanistan might be used to give Pakistan strategic depth emerged early in Pakistan's history, and came to be advocated in particular by General Mirza Aslam Beg, who became chief of army staff after Zia's death and who advocates the idea to this day.[10]

The broad idea seems to be that in the event of an Indian attack, the Hindu Kush mountain range would provide a barrier behind which Pakistani forces could regroup. But it is a baffling idea in military terms. Just as the Hindu Kush and the mountainous and inhospitable FATA regions might provide a shield, so would they also present a formidable obstacle to land forces trying to conduct a strategic withdrawal. If it is the air force that is expected to benefit most, this would require suitable runways and shelters on the Afghan side and, in any case, the mountains would be no greater obstacle to attacking forces than to the withdrawing defenders. The concept therefore seems to derive most of its power from its non-military associations. By appealing to the affinity between Pashtuns on either side of the Durand Line and, more widely, between Muslim Afghanistan and Muslim Pakistan, it promotes the notion of a commonality of interest against Hindu India, and may also be intended to dilute the force of Pashtun nationalism.

Ironically, in the light of its ultimate failure to win over either the Afghan populace or successive Afghan governments, Pakistan has, if anything, found itself providing strategic depth for Afghanistan's Taliban and other insurgents.

But in 1980, such unintended outcomes were as yet remote. Despite their very different perspectives on the region, Pakistan and the West had a joint interest in forcing a Soviet withdrawal, and they shared a willingness to make use of religion for this purpose. The religious element was also strongly supported by the Saudis, who matched US aid to Pakistan dollar for dollar.[11]

The rationale seems to have been that the most effective direct instrument for dealing with the invaders would be the Afghan people themselves, who knew the terrain and had a tradition of fighting. Arms, training and 'advisers' were thus supplied to Afghanistan in great volume. But, given the asymmetry of the battle, the real key to success would be motivation. Pakistan and the US concluded that the most effective force multipliers would be the Afghan fighters' religious convictions and tribal customs. And indeed, tribal custom, in which collective and personal honour demand that anyone who violates the integrity of the home territory be forcibly evicted, combined with the Muslim idea of jihad, or holy war, to stir Afghanistan's mullahs and maliks (religious and tribal leaders respectively) to lead an armed defiance of the foreign invader. Whatever the faith of individual Soviet soldiers – among whom there would no doubt have been many Muslims – as a group, they were characterised by these Afghan fighters as unbelievers, or infidels. This meant that any Muslim who entered the fight against them could be honoured with the label mujahid, or holy warrior. If he were to die in battle, he would go straight to paradise and enjoy its many rewards.

With strong religious 'force multipliers' thus in evidence, it suited the US and Pakistani leaderships to work with the grain of opinion in Afghanistan, to support the mujahadeen, and to motivate resistance. Also helping to feed the jihadist current was Pakistan's Jamaat-e-Islami (JI) party, which saw the jihad in Afghanistan as an opportunity to spread the Islamic revolution to the Soviet Union's Central Asian republics.[12]

Zia had several objectives that he believed could be advanced through cooperation with the US and militant groups which did not coincide with US interests. These included the consolidation of his own power and, by extension, that of the army; the encouragement of the Islamisation of Pakistan, including through the revision of educational curricula;[13] and a reduction in Indian influence in the region. He particularly wanted to ensure that at the end of the conflict there would be in place an Afghan regime that was duly grateful to Pakistan and accordingly compliant and supportive, and that would, by offering stability on Pakistan's western border, bolster Pakistan's strength in the context of its rivalry with India.[14] But no such regime emerged: the main beneficiary of Zia's efforts to produce one was the Hezb-i-Islami Afghanistan (Afghanistan Islamic Party) led by the notorious warlord Gulbuddin Hekmatyar.[15]

Attracted by the religious cause, and encouraged by several governments, men came from several different countries to join the jihad: from Saudi Arabia, Yemen and Palestine, even from the neighbouring Soviet republics of Turkmenistan and Uzbekistan. They were supplemented by young Pakistani men who had been trained and motivated in the madrasas that had proliferated in the northwest of the country with the help of extensive finance from Saudi Arabia and elsewhere in the Gulf. Assisted by the West and hardened over nearly a decade of battle, over the course of the 1980s, the mujahadeen developed into a formidable fighting force with immense resourcefulness and powers of endurance. When the Soviets finally withdrew in 1989, Afghanistan and Pakistan were replete with fighters and weaponry. Pakistan's army and intelligence forces had gained confidence, influence and strength. And Zia had accelerated Pakistan's nuclear-weapons programme.[16]

The alliance breaks down: the Taliban emerges

As soon as the Soviets left, the US took the view that its strategic objective had been achieved, and the US relationship with Pakistan changed dramatically. In 1990, declaring that it could no longer be certain that Pakistan was not developing nuclear weapons, the George H.W. Bush administration reimposed the sanctions that had been lifted a decade earlier when the balance of interests had been different. Military assistance and financial aid to Pakistan were halted. Pakistani military officers ceased to be trained in the US.

But the US did nothing to address the consequences of having built up a fighting force driven by religious fervour, just as it did nothing to stabilise Afghan governance systems.[17] So long as they were busy in Afghanistan, the mujahadeen had presented little threat outside that country. But once their mission of ejecting the Soviets had been accomplished, they became a substantial and vigorous cadre of men very ready to use their skills, experience and zeal in the service of similar causes elsewhere. Though Zia's death in 1988 and the election of Benazir Bhutto as prime minister shortly after brought an end to direct influence and support for the mujahadeen from the Pakistani leadership, significant elements of the group's sustaining infrastructure remained in place in the form of funding and assistance from the ISI. In 1971, there had been around 900 madrasas in Pakistan. By 1988, thanks to funding from the ISI and sources in Saudi Arabia and the Gulf, there were around 8,000 official religious schools and an estimated 25,000 unregistered ones.[18]

It was around this time, at the end of the 1980s, that Kashmir, which had been relatively calm since the 1971 war with India, experienced a period of exceptional turmoil and violence. In the absence of progress on addressing Kashmiri grievances, anti-Indian opinion had hardened over the course of the decade, and several Pakistani militant groups had become increasingly active in the Kashmir Valley. They found ready partners among the newly available fighters from the Afghan war, who were encouraged by the ISI to transfer their attentions and activities to the 'freedom struggle' in Kashmir. With the ISI's help and training and ISI-supplied weapons and finance, mujahadeen were infiltrated across the 'Line of Control'[19] dividing the Pakistani-administered and Indian-administered parts of Kashmir to stimulate insurgency and conduct sabotage on the Indian side. Some went on to penetrate India beyond the state of Jammu and Kashmir. However, it became clear that, while the ISI could help to make such fighters more effective, here as in Afghanistan, there were limits to the control it could exert. This was to prove the pattern for the next two decades.

Meanwhile, Afghanistan no longer attracted international attention and was left to its own devices by those countries outside the region that had taken such a close interest during the Soviet occupation. Focusing instead on Saddam Hussein's August 1990 invasion of Kuwait, Western governments failed to appreciate that the power vacuum left in Afghanistan following the Soviet withdrawal and the attendant violent political turmoil were to lead to another, very different strategic challenge. It should perhaps have been foreseeable that armed and trained groups of religious zealots were unlikely to disperse peaceably the moment a particular set of Western objectives had been achieved.

During this period of neglect, Afghanistan virtually disintegrated[20] and became dominated by competing warlords. At the end of 1994, the Taliban movement emerged under the leadership of 35-year-old Mullah Mohammad Omar. The group, whose name means 'students', was mostly made up of former mujahadeen and young Afghans who had studied at radical madrasas in Pakistan. It was initially viewed benignly by the US, and welcomed in Afghanistan itself for its opposition to the criminalities and brutalities of the warlords. The group built up its appeal further over the course of the 1990s with the cultivation of a heroic narrative that portrayed it as having restored stability and just governance, while seeking no reward for itself.[21]

Like other observers, Pakistan had been dismayed by the rise of the Afghan warlords, and had become increasingly concerned about the prospect of anarchy within its western neighbour. This concern prompted it to actively help consolidate Mullah Omar's position. From 1994 to 1996, General Naseerullah Babar, a minister in Benazir Bhutto's second government, having failed to win over the warlords, did much to help the Taliban defeat them. Pakistan supplied advice and ex-services personnel to the Taliban, and was instrumental in the group's capture of a large arms dump from warlords. But Babar was as mistaken as so many others when he calculated that the Taliban – 'our boys', as he called them – could be induced to support Pakistan's interests.[22] In his own words, Mullah Omar's purpose was to take up 'arms to achieve the aims of the Afghan jihad and save our people from further suffering at the hands of the so-called mujahadeen'.[23] The Taliban frequently made clear their independence of Pakistan by, for instance, insisting that Pakistan not bypass them when sending convoys into Afghanistan, and demanding that it cease cutting deals with others.

The Taliban's increasingly idiosyncratic and violent behaviour over the course of the 1990s and their connections with terrorism eventually alienated international opinion. Following the al-Qaeda bombings of US embassies in Kenya and Tanzania in August 1998, the US progressively pressured the regime and imposed sanctions. The US and British governments withdrew their officials from Afghanistan, and discouraged their citizens from entering or doing business with the country. In February 1999, the UK suspended funding to non-governmental organisations employing British staff on the ground in Afghanistan,[24] on the grounds that it had become impossible to safely conduct development programmes in the country. But danger on the ground seldom necessitates the withdrawal of all officials from a country and complete cessation of contact. It would seem, therefore, that these policies were driven less by safety considerations than by an aversion to dealing, even indirectly, with a regime such as the Taliban, and by a sense of a need to be seen to be recognising the problematic nature of the regime.

Such gestures had no influence on the Taliban themselves. But the UK's withdrawal of funding to NGOs was deeply unpopular among those organisations that chose to continue working in Afghanistan. Not only did it mean that many groups lost their funding: they also suffered from the absence of an official US or UK presence on the ground. From the governments' side, officials were to come to feel the lack of interaction with an established expert population of private and voluntary-sector personnel – journalists, businesspeople and aid workers – based in Afghanistan. With the reduced presence of NGOs, up-to-date Western knowledge and understanding of Afghanistan and the personalities active there rapidly eroded. The absence of officials and experts in the country also meant that it was difficult for Western powers to distinguish between what Pakistan was saying it was doing in relation to Afghanistan and the reality on the ground.

It was during this period of Taliban ascendancy that al-Qaeda established itself in Afghanistan, subsequently infecting Pakistan and elsewhere. In an interview in early 2009, the director general of the British Security Service, Jonathan Evans, stating that the main threats to the UK came from al-Qaeda's core in Pakistan and its assets in the UK, observed that in the years before 2001, al-Qaeda had been 'able to establish terrorist training facilities [in Afghanistan] and to draw in hardened extremists and vulnerable recruits to indoctrinate and teach techniques'.[25] When the handful of academics, UN diplomats, journalists and aid workers who had kept in touch with developments had expressed increasing concern about what was happening in the country in these years, their warnings had fallen on deaf ears. This wilful neglect was to have a great cost.

Meanwhile, successive Pakistani governments, joined only by Saudi Arabia and the United Arab Emirates, recognised the Taliban as the government of Afghanistan and continued to support them even after it had become clear that they had become little better than the warlords they had supplanted. In March 2001, six months before the 11 September attacks, the Taliban destroyed the 1,500-year-old giant statues of the Buddha at Bamiyan, causing outrage throughout the world. It was perhaps this event more than any other that brought the focus of international attention back onto events in Afghanistan, including the massive stockpiling of opium and the escalating poverty of hundreds of thousands of people.

Pakistan itself could hardly be unaware of such problems, having become home to some three million Afghan refugees from both the Taliban regime and earlier turmoil, who filled makeshift camps and swelled urban populations from Peshawar in the north to Karachi in the south. In February 2001, the author of this book asked Musharraf if he was not concerned that, in continuing to support an increasingly out-of-control Taliban, he might be riding a tiger that could come to threaten Pakistan's own security. While Musharraf's own response was equivocal, a close adviser confessed that Taliban behaviour had indeed begun to cause great concern, but that Pakistan's attempts to moderate it were having no impact; indeed, they were being met with humiliating rebuffs. After several fruitless visits to Mullah Omar, Pakistani government minister General Moinuddin Haider finally resorted to enlisting a number of learned clerics to argue from scripture against Omar's religious justifications of various Taliban policies, in an effort to persuade Mullah Omar that the group's behaviour was un-Islamic. Omar dismissed the move, saying that Afghanistan had its own *shura* (assembly of scholars and advisers), and had no need of outside interference.[26]

In his 2006 autobiography, Musharraf rather disingenuously discusses Pakistan's attitude to the Taliban, implying that the group's emergence was inevitable and that Pakistan had no option but to have dealings with it, and omitting any critical reference to Pakistan's active role in its creation or Pakistan's failure, until too late, to influence or control it. 'The Taliban were not a new, post-Soviet phenomenon', the former president observes, 'they were taught by the same teachers in the same seminaries that had produced the mujahadeen'. Furthermore: 'We have strong ethnic and family linkages with the Taliban. The opponent of the Taliban was the Northern Alliance, composed of Tajiks, Uzbeks and Hazaras, backed by Russia, India and Iran. How could any Pakistani government be favourably inclined toward the Northern Alliance?'[27] This is surely little different from saying that 'my enemy's enemy is my friend'.

Pakistan's attention in the late 1990s was not exclusively focused on the challenges on its western flank. As in the 1980s and now, Pakistan's interests in Afghanistan in this period were intermingled with its concerns about India. The same line of Pakistani-sponsored mujahadeen who had originated in the Afghanistan war, gone on to support the Pakistani cause in Kashmir and subsequently fought with or, if they sided with the warlords, against the Taliban, participated in Pakistan's notorious Kargil offensive in Kashmir in 1999. In a mission instigated by Musharraf as chief of army staff with the approval of Prime Minister Nawaz Sharif, the Pakistan Northern Light Infantry and Army Special Forces, disguised as non-military 'freedom fighters', seized strategic high ground in the Kargil and Drass region of Indian-administered Kashmir which, at 15,000 feet, dominated an important Indian supply road. This provoked several months of limited conflict in the region.[28] The Pakistani claim that the action was initiated by 'thousands of mujahadeen, mostly indigenous to Kashmir but also supported by freelance sympathisers from Pakistan'[29] was not credible to anyone familiar with the Pakistani army's strong presence in that region. This adventure, involving two countries that had declared their possession of nuclear weapons less than a year earlier, represented a striking example of reckless misjudgement on the part of the Pakistani leadership, and Musharraf in particular. Sharif was forced to back down by US President Bill Clinton on American Independence Day, and the ensuing recriminations between Sharif and Musharraf paved the way for Musharraf's coup later that year.

When al-Qaeda attacked targets in New York and Washington in 2001 in an operation that had its origins in Afghanistan, Musharraf was forced finally to repudiate the Taliban. As it once again needed Pakistan's cooperation to pursue its interests in Afghanistan, the US in effect renewed the relationship it had established in 1980 following the Soviet invasion. A wide range of US sanctions, including those imposed in 1998 in response to India's and Pakistan's nuclear tests and others imposed after Musharraf's coup, were suspended. The delivery of massive quantities of aid to Pakistan, the great majority of it military, was resumed. Pakistan became a coalition partner in what the George W. Bush administration called the 'global war on terror'. This time, the common enemy included many who both countries had supported 20 years earlier.

However it did not follow, in Pakistani opinion, that support for Kashmiri 'freedom fighters', whom much of the rest of the world regarded as terrorists, would cease as a result. In December 2001, an attack on the Indian parliament caused outrage in India and led to the mobilisation of the Indian Army. Musharraf distanced Pakistan from the attack and described it as an act of terrorism. But just as Musharraf could not control but did not wish to break with the Taliban until he was forced to do so following the 11 September attacks, he steadfastly refused to disband militant groups in Kashmir during a ten-month-long dangerous stand-off with India in which both countries' armies were mobilised. From Pakistan's perspective, these groups, which the ISI had helped to train, were valuable irregulars who could supplement Pakistani security forces in the event of war with India. So long as they could be kept occupied, either on the eastern border harassing India, or on the western border engaged in Afghanistan, they would be ready for full mobilisation whenever necessary.

There has therefore been a direct connection, in the form of the mujahadeen originally created by Pakistan and the West in the 1980s, between the violence and conflict in Afghanistan in the 1980s, the escalation of the Kashmir conflict from 1989–99, the emergence of India and Pakistan as overt nuclear-weapons powers in 1998, and the tensions between Pakistan and India of 2001–02. From the start of US operations in Afghanistan in October 2001 up until 2003, when Pakistan's relations with India eased, Pakistan felt itself to be subject to threats on two fronts simultaneously: from al-Qaeda and Pakistan's former allies the Taliban in the west, and from the Indian Army in the east. Even after the immediate crisis with India passed, Pakistan considered India to be acting against it in Afghanistan.

Pakistan's army and its intelligence services were closely involved in the events described above. However, the role played by these institutions has been a product of the strategic judgements of the army itself, not of disinterested assessments of the broader national interest. A perennial priority for the military in its analyses of the strategic situation has been the advantage of the military institution itself. Strong at the outset, and strengthened by extensive external support, the Pakistani army has become the most powerful and effective institution in the country. Other states have displayed little understanding of Pakistan's complexities in this and other matters, and have made serious mistakes in their relationships with the country as a result. The West's understandable exasperation with the army's double-dealing and dangerous adventurism has complicated relations with Pakistan, compounding the difficulties for all parties of managing an ongoing tense and intricate regional situation. As a result, the army places little store by Western values and expectations. This is not new: long before the US departed the scene in 1989, Pakistan's army concluded that it would set its own moral and strategic compass, largely independently of the strategic and political concerns of the country's civilian politicians.

Politics in the 1990s: between two generals

Since the death of General Zia-ul-Haq in 1988, civilian politics in Pakistan has been dominated by two political families, the Bhuttos and the Sharifs. The Bhutto power base is in Sindh province, while the Sharif industrial empire is in Punjab. Smaller regional parties play an important role as coalition partners for the larger parties. The street power of the Muttahida Qaumi Movement (MQM) in Karachi, for example, can seldom be ignored by those forging political alliances, though it frequently brings with it extreme violence. The Awami National Party (ANP) has traditionally dominated NWFP. Though religious parties have seldom attracted even a tenth of the vote in Pakistan, in 2002, the first-past-the-post electoral system combined with the help of Musharraf's fixers meant that the 11% share of the vote won nationally by the Muttahida Majlis-e-Amal (MMA, United Action Front) religious alliance enabled it to oust the ANP from NWFP and become a significant part of the government in Baluchistan as well. But even in 2002, when both party leaders were barred from participating in the election, Benazir Bhutto's and Nawaz Sharif's parties were the main civilian political forces at the national level. Neither has an inspiring history.

Having taken up the mantle of her father, Zulfikar Ali Bhutto, as leader of the Pakistan People's Party (PPP), Benazir Bhutto became prime minister in a coalition led by the PPP in 1988. Dismissed by President Ghulam Ishaq Khan in 1990, she became prime minister again in 1994 and was again dismissed, this time by a different president, Farooq Leghari, in 1996.

Nawaz Sharif fared no better. The Islamic Democratic Alliance (IJI), of which Sharif's Pakistan Muslim League (PML) faction was a key component,[30] was established in 1998 with the help of the political wing of the ISI[31] to counter Bhutto's PPP. Though not an Islamist party, the alliance had an expressly Islamic social agenda, in a conscious echo of Zia's emphasis on religion.[32] It won power in November 1990 following Bhutto's dismissal. But Sharif's government too was dismissed, by Ghulam Ishaq Khan in 1993, after only two-and-a-half years in office. The PML nonetheless went on win again in 1997, with a narrow margin, following Bhutto's second dismissal. Sharif's second tenure came to an end with Musharraf's coup in 1999. The records of the second terms of both Bhutto's and Sharif's governments were worse than their disappointing first terms.

Writing in the late 1990s, South Asia historian Ian Talbot remarked of the period that 'Pakistan had become a zero-sum game, in which oppositions denied ruling parties any legitimacy and governments used selective accountability to harry and intimidate their opponents. Parliament was at worst a bear pit, at best the fountainhead of patronage politics, with legislation being restricted to presidential ordinance.'[33] The description might equally be applied to the conduct of party politics in the Musharraf years.

On each of the three occasions on which presidents dismissed elected governments, they did so using a special power that had been introduced by Zia, Article 58(2)b of the Eighth Amendment of the Constitution. Whatever the specific justifications of its use – and in each case, these appear to have been substantial – the provision is, unsurprisingly, controversial among the political parties. Indeed, dispute over it continues between Sharif and current President Asif Ali Zardari.

The reasons for the premature ends of four successive elected governments are various, convoluted and, of course, hotly disputed. The two presidents and the general responsible for the dismissals made serious accusations in each case. Those accused contested these, made counter-accusations and declared that subsequent elections were rigged. Since few of the allegations were tested in court, and since the judiciary was itself often implicated or suspect in other ways, there can be little certainty about rights and wrongs. However, it is part of the tragedy of Pakistan's experience with electoral politics that hindsight and examination by disinterested observers suggest that both accusations and counter-accusations are likely to have been well founded.

The specific charges laid against Benazir Bhutto and Nawaz Sharif in relation to their time in government have been extensively and authoritatively explored elsewhere. But whatever their precise foundations in fact, many of the allegations of corruption and violence have come to be believed by large segments of the electorate, and these beliefs continue to influence political processes. In addition, though Bhutto herself was assassinated in 2007, many of the political figures active in the period of elected civilian rule between the Zia and Musharraf regimes, including Nawaz Sharif, his brother Shahbaz, and Bhutto's husband Asif Ali Zardari, remain major players today. The animosity between the two main parties is as evident as ever. Since the past, in these respects, has a bearing on the present, it is useful to highlight some aspects of the political history of the 1990s that may be relevant today. When scrutinising the records of those involved, it is salutary to bear in mind that Pakistan's inherent tensions, combined with the external and economic challenges it faces – among them, admittedly, many of Pakistan's own making – render it an extraordinarily difficult country to govern. Governance has been made all the more difficult by the fact that each of the leaders concerned has set out with relatively little practical experience of government.

Bhutto's first term

When Benazir Bhutto took office in 1988, Western educated, the first female and the youngest prime minister in Pakistan's history, she faced enormous expectations of her leadership. In any circumstances, these would have been unfulfillable. As it was, the army had ensured that Zia's foreign minister would be retained in Bhutto's cabinet, and the president, Ghulam Ishaq Khan, was close to the army. Thus, although not directly in power, the army was politically entrenched and could readily exercise its influence.[34] This arrangement rendered Bhutto the least powerful of the troika of president, chief of army staff and prime minister. Meanwhile, Nawaz Sharif was using his power base in Punjab as a launching pad for attacks on Bhutto's government. Bitter infighting within and between the main parties became increasingly personalised. Bhutto's own power base in Sindh was riven with ethnic, sectarian and criminally motivated violence. The PPP's coalition partner, the MQM, defected and became a fierce opponent. Bhutto reacted to these challenges intemperately. In an atmosphere of mounting violence and political disorder, it was Bhutto's attempt to defy the army over military appointments and its demands for increased powers in Sindh that precipitated her undoing.

Ghulam Ishaq Khan's grounds for Bhutto's first dismissal were that she had lost the capacity to govern, demonstrated an inability to stem violence, and nurtured nepotism and corrupt practices by family members and associates.[35] Later, a special court ordered that she stand trial on charges of corruption and misconduct. In October 1990, Bhutto's husband was arrested and charged with kidnapping a Pakistani-born British citizen, from whom he was accused of having extorted a large sum of money. The caretaker government that had taken office following Bhutto's dismissal earlier that year claimed that she had paid an American publicist nearly half a million dollars to improve her image. Bhutto fiercely contested this and the other allegations. But the PPP lost ground in every province in the ensuing election, even failing to gain a simple majority in Bhutto's home province of Sindh.

Bhutto's premiership had comprehensively failed to live up to expectations. This was partly due to the constraints upon her power. But it was also a consequence of her government's preference for patronage and confrontation over principle, and its apparent unwillingness to make any attempt to build consensus with other political forces.[36]

Sharif's first term

In contrast to Bhutto's feudal roots in rural Sindh, Nawaz Sharif came from a self-made industrial family. He also had close ties to the army, having been appointed Zia's chief minister in Punjab at the instigation of his father.[37] His family bore a deep grudge against the Bhutto family because of Zulfikar's nationalisation of part of the Sharif industrial empire; this was restored to the family by Zia after Sharif's father pledged his support.

It was just before Bhutto's dismissal in 1990 that the US decided to cut off economic and military aid and reintroduce sanctions because of concerns about nuclear proliferation. Paradoxically, and despite US denials, this move was viewed by many in Pakistan as an attempt to assist the PPP and counter the Islamic-leaning IJI opposition coalition. There has been speculation that this perception helped the IJI in the general election that year.[38] In any event, the IJI, led by Sharif, won the poll convincingly.

Sharif had the advantage over Bhutto that his coalition achieved a solid majority and his party had a secure power base in Punjab. He was also more adept at patronage, and he combined his business interests with a strong religious commitment, thereby appealing to diverse interest groups. But these attributes also had their drawbacks, and criticism over them dogged both his governments. Sharif was accused of favouring commercial and banking interests at the expense of the poor. And while some denounced what they claimed was a programme to convert Pakistan into a theocratic state, religious groups complained of a lack of commitment to Islamic principles.[39] Sharif also suffered from the official policy, established by the preceding caretaker administration, of opposing Saddam Hussein's invasion of Kuwait. This and his refusal to support Gulbuddin Hekmatyar in the Afghan power struggle contributed to the withdrawal of influential religious party the JI from his coalition in 1992.[40] As Sharif struggled to satisfy these divergent interests, Pakistan's relations with the US deteriorated sharply. In 1993, the country was placed on a list of potential terrorist-supporting states for six months and subjected to further sanctions for allegedly violating the Missile Technology Control Regime.

Meanwhile, violence in Sindh, corruption claims and political confrontation continued under Sharif as under Bhutto. The two party leaders appeared to be pursuing a personal vendetta against each other.[41] When President Khan complained that the government was engaged in extensive corruption, making arbitrary assaults on the opposition, and using privatisation as a pretext for indulging in secret business deals and pay-offs, the president's relationship with Sharif, already strained, reached breaking point. This presented Bhutto with a potential opportunity to ally with Sharif to trim the powers of the president who had dismissed her. But she decided to take her revenge on Sharif instead, and sided with the president. Sharif's petition against his dismissal was upheld by the Supreme Court, prompting outrage and a constitutional crisis. It took the intervention of the chief of the army staff to defuse the situation by persuading both the president and Sharif to resign, and the country went to the polls yet again.[42] Bhutto had the additional satisfaction of seeing her hitherto vilified husband, Zardari, inducted into the caretaker government that followed Sharif's departure.[43]

Bhutto's second term

Neither party achieved a majority in the 1993 election. Bhutto's PPP gained more seats in the National Assembly than Sharif's PML(Nawaz) (the dominant faction of the PML to emerge following a split in the party as a result of the constitutional crisis described above), while the PML(N) gained slightly more of the popular vote, in a turnout well below 50%.[44] Nevertheless, Bhutto succeeded in forming a coalition, and took power pledging to revitalise the country, heal wounds and begin a process of reconciliation. Unusually, the PPP had achieved electoral dominance in Punjab as well as Sindh and this combined with the success of the PPP candidate for president, Farooq Leghari, meant that for a time, such a process of renewal seemed possible. Hopes were high that lessons had been learned and that as a result, Pakistani politics might have matured.

But it was not to be. Inheriting an impoverished economy and facing no diminution in inter-party rivalry, Bhutto reverted to a style familiar from her first tenure. Pakistan's international position was weakened by concerns about its nuclear-weapons capability, its purchase of missiles from China, and its apparent involvement in Kashmiri terrorism and a Sikh insurrection in the Indian state of Punjab. In addition, feuding between members of the Bhutto family, involving Benazir's mother, Nusrat, and her brother, Murtaza, over the leadership of the Bhutto clan, in which Benazir's husband was deeply and deviously involved, led to violence and death.

Party politics in this period came to involve more than power struggles and the gathering of spoils, degenerating into a sequence of organised clandestine attacks on and assassinations of political opponents.[45] In 1995, the discovery of an army plot to oust Bhutto and the resulting turmoil led the chief of the army staff to stand down. By this time, despite having been Bhutto's choice for the post, the new president was plainly distancing himself from her. Unconfirmed press allegations that Zardari had bought a 350-acre estate in Surrey, England, for £2.7m in addition to properties in Belgravia in London, and that he had transferred funds from Karachi to Guernsey,[46] had a huge political impact. This impact was made even greater by the coincidence of the reports with criticism of Pakistan's economic management by the IMF.[47] Murtaza Bhutto, having set up a breakaway party, launched furious attacks on Benazir and on Zardari's alleged corruption. In September 1996, Murtaza was shot dead by a police contingent near his home in Karachi in bizarre circumstances, the day after he had registered complaints that the government was blocking his political activities. His widow accused Zardari of having arranged her husband's assassination. Before Murtaza's death, his mother had claimed that her daughter's husband intended to destroy the Bhutto clan in order to inherit its legacy.

Five days after Murtaza's assassination and following discussions with Sharif, President Leghari publicly alluded to the possibility of using his special powers, in view of the state of the nation, to dismiss the government and dissolve the parliamentary assemblies. Five weeks later, on 5 November, he did so, amid violent anti-government demonstrations. He cited the climate of violence, manipulation of the judicial system, political interference with official appointments, the use of inappropriate methods to neutralise opposition, nepotism and the critical state of the economy. He also ordered the arrest of Zardari, who at the time was federal minister for investment.

Demonstrations aside, the Pakistani public and foreign opinion reacted fairly calmly to all this turbulence. Both appeared to have grown indifferent to the country's political strife, and to feel little dismay or shock. The US State Department, which had initially had high hopes for Bhutto's second term, stated simply that the problems were an internal matter for Pakistan, and that the president appeared to have acted within his constitutional authority.

Sharif's second term: prelude to a coup

The election that followed in early 1997 had an even lower turnout than the 1993 poll, around 26%. The overwhelming majority of seats, some two-thirds, fell to Sharif's PML(N), which became the first party to gain an overall majority since 1984. Bhutto's PPP was trounced.

However, the two-and-a-half-year Sharif prime ministership that ensued was perhaps the most disastrous of all the four elected governments since Zia. Sharif's populist and business-friendly public-expenditure projects – among them the construction of a rarely used toll road between Lahore and Islamabad and an 'own-your-own' taxicab scheme he had begun in his first term – set the country on the path to bankruptcy. But even more damaging were his across-the-board attempts to modify the country's already weak institutions so as to enhance his own influence. The national Ehtesab (Reform) Commission, tasked with investigating corruption allegations, was used selectively, primarily to pursue Sharif's political opponents. These included Benazir Bhutto who, though convicted of corruption, was allowed to flee to London, where she would pose less of a political threat than if she were in prison in Pakistan.[48] Sharif forced President Leghari to resign, installed a cipher in his place and caused the newcomer to acquiesce in a constitutional amendment that removed the president's power to dismiss parliament and, hence, the prime minister.

Sharif also purged the bureaucracy, bullied the press to the extent of having journalists arrested and beaten up, manipulated local elections and meddled in the appointment of judges. At the end of 1997, his supporters invaded the Supreme Court in Islamabad and intimidated judges hearing a case in which he was a defendant.[49] In October 1998, he secured the passage through the National Assembly of a bill to amend the constitution so as to make sharia law the supreme law in Pakistan.[50] Had the bill not been rejected in the upper house, its passage would have represented a massive victory for the Islamic radicals whom Sharif had always courted. But Sharif may have been motivated more by the possibility that the amendment would have rendered the prime minister, himself, the *amir al-Momineen*, or final arbiter of disputes, a role that entails substantial temporal, as well as religious, authority.[51]

In the midst of all this, in the spring of 1998, India surprised the world by conducting a series of nuclear tests and declaring that it had a nuclear-weapons capability. Pakistan, which had made sure that it would be ready for such an eventuality, responded with tests of its own and a similar declaration.

The army, like other elements of Pakistani society, witnessed the country's economic decline, violence and widespread corruption with mounting concern. The moderate and principled Chief of Army Staff General Jehangir Karamat resisted the many calls that were made on him to halt Sharif's excesses by intervening directly. Instead, he proposed the establishment of a National Security Council that would have widened the consultative and decision-making process for dealing with internal challenges, as well as external national security issues. Sharif's response to what was to him an unwelcome proposal was ultimately to be his undoing.

In October 1998, Sharif forced Karamat to resign, but it was not long before he also fell out with Karamat's successor, Pervez Musharraf. The army was incensed by Sharif's signature of an agreement with Indian Prime Minister Atal Behari Vajpayee during Vajpayee's visit to Pakistan in February 1999. The Lahore Declaration, which was aimed at resuming bilateral discussions, paid insufficient regard, in the army's view, to Pakistan's interests in Kashmir. Soon after it was signed, Musharraf initiated the politically disastrous Kargil operation, the planning for which must have been in train at the time of Vajpayee's conciliatory visit. Musharraf was then further infuriated by Sharif's subsequent claim to have had no prior knowledge of the operation and by his humiliating climbdown under pressure from President Clinton, which in Musharraf's view squandered the opportunity to negotiate Indian concessions in exchange for a ceasefire.

That autumn, having carefully prepared the ground, Sharif tried to replace Musharraf with a nominee of his own while the general was away on official business in Sri Lanka. But Musharraf had anticipated something like this, and Sharif was forced to resign at gunpoint in October 1999.[52] He was imprisoned for a year before being exiled to Saudi Arabia. His departure was not mourned by the citizenry.

* * *

The four elected governments in the decade preceding the army's third takeover have a number of features in common. Throughout the period, as discussed, the army was never truly absent from politics. On matters of national security, including nuclear weapons, and on key foreign-policy issues such as India, Afghanistan and Kashmir, the army never ceded control of policy and operations to civilian authorities,[53] with the role of government departments such as the foreign ministry in these fields largely confined to taking instruction and gathering material for arguments to make in defence of army-directed policies. Always alert to possible damage to their own institutional interests, the army and the ISI frequently manipulated the political process and rigged votes in favour of their supporters and against their detractors.

Fierce rivalry between the two main parties was another common feature, in evidence from the very start of Bhutto's first prime ministership, in conjunction with ruthless political opportunism. Violence, nepotism and patronage took the place of ideology. Coalitions with minority parties frequently collapsed in acrimony. At street level, lawlessness and violence were prevalent across the country, especially in Sindh and Baluchistan. Democratic participation declined over the period, with turnout in the four elections between 1988 and 1997 falling from 50% in 1988 to around 26% in 1997. Musharraf's 1999 coup of course required no one but the army to turn out. But there is no doubt about its popularity at the time.[54]

There were other commonalities between the Bhutto and Sharif governments. Neither administration introduced any significant reforms. Both ran up huge debts, well beyond the profligacies of Zulfikar Ali Bhutto and Zia. Many of the funds under their control have never been accounted for. The two leaders – each from multimillionaire families – were both accused of corruption, and both claimed that their accusers were politically motivated. Corruption is endemic in Pakistani politics, partly because of the perceived need to use large inducements to secure support. But the Sharif and Bhutto eras saw this corrosive problem reach unprecedented heights.

The Musharraf era: early reforms

On 12 October 1999, Sharif ordered that General Musharraf's plane, on its way back from Sri Lanka, be prevented from landing in Pakistan. In line with plans drawn up for such a contingency, the army enabled the general to land in Karachi, thereby possibly saving his life, as the plane was short of fuel. Sharif was arrested by military personnel and forced to resign. Following this bloodless coup, Musharraf installed himself as 'chief executive' of the nation.

The British and US governments were quick to condemn Musharraf's action, their position encapsulated in the words of British Foreign Minister Robin Cook: 'There is no such thing as a good coup.'[55] Both countries imposed sanctions in addition to those in place since the 1998 nuclear tests. In the case of the UK, development assistance to Pakistan, hitherto immune to sanctions, was halted.

In contrast, Sharif's departure was widely welcomed in Pakistan itself. Musharraf capitalised on Sharif's unpopularity and reputation for corruption, and distanced himself from the radical Islamist tendencies associated with the former prime minister, extolling instead the secularist model offered by Turkey, where he had lived as a boy. In May 2000, the Supreme Court declared Musharraf's takeover to be valid, citing a controversial 'Doctrine of Necessity'. It also stipulated that elections should be held before October 2002. Reluctantly, Musharraf promised to conform to this timetable. An adept public speaker, he pledged to bring about a modern, moderate Muslim state and introduced a series of institutional reforms to this end.

Under Musharraf, the Ehtesab Commission, which Sharif had used to investigate allegations of corruption made against his enemies, became the National Accountability Bureau (NAB). It focused in particular on Sharif and Bhutto. However, it had little success in bringing prosecutions, as admissible evidence proved hard to come by, though current Prime Minister Yousuf Gilani was convicted of corruption in 2004 following a prosecution brought by the NAB. (The ruling was overturned by the High Court in February 2009.)[56] The bureau had more success recouping funds through plea bargaining. Most significantly, however, the threat of financial scrutiny the body represented gave it coercive influence over the civilian political process. The NAB was doubly unpopular because serving military officers were exempt from its remit. The fact that, on one occasion, a retired navy chief was able to escape further action from the commission by settling out of court with a payment of $7.5m suggested that the military itself was hardly immune to corruption.

Musharraf made no secret of his personal contempt for Bhutto and Sharif, and indeed for civilian politicians in general. Believing, like many of his military colleagues, that politicians as a group had let the country down, he declared his intention to cultivate a new generation of elected politicians who would emerge from 'the people', rather than from what was viewed as the tainted pool of the traditional parties. A new, third tier of government was established, intended to under-pin the existing national and provincial assemblies. Beginning in December 2000, elections were held for new local assemblies, headed by elected *nazim*, or mayors, who would receive development funding directly from the central government. A National Reconstruction Bureau (NRB), to be led by workaholic lieutenant-general Tanvir Naqvi, was established to coordinate the establishment of the assemblies. Musharraf claimed that the scheme would break the stranglehold of the bureaucracy and self-serving national and provincial politicians on development and poverty-alleviation efforts at the local level.

With the country nearly bankrupt following years of profligacy, Musharraf gave high priority to economic reform and appointed a senior Citibank executive, Shaukat Aziz, as finance minister, supporting him vigorously over the introduction of unpopular measures.

The deterioration of public education had started under Zia, but the sector had also been sorely neglected by Bhutto and Sharif. Sharif, in particular, was believed to have used educational appointments as political inducements, leading to cohorts of 'ghost teachers' who drew salaries but failed to appear in classrooms. Villages equipped with school buildings, many of which were also the products of patronage, saw these stand empty as a result. Musharraf markedly increased financial allocations to education, albeit from a low base, and appointed as education minister a woman from Baluchistan, signalling a recognition of the importance both of female education and of improving the extremely low literacy rate in that province.

Like other generals before him, Musharraf was careful to stress his wish to see a return to democracy as soon as practicable. After much prompting from Western governments, he eventually produced a 'road map to democracy', which outlined a series of steps that would lead to elections. In contrast to Sharif's attempts to gag the press, Musharraf was tolerant of criticism, of which there was plenty, in English-language newspapers and, at least initially, on the burgeoning satellite television channels. The vernacular press, which is much more widely read and generally far more radical on religious matters, exercised – with some encouragement – more self-censorship. Internet access and usage, hitherto almost non-existent, soared.

Some of Musharraf's more ambitious reforms proved difficult to implement. For instance, a general was put in charge of the new National Database and Registration Authority (NADRA) tasked with introducing national identity cards for every citizen. Foreign diplomats were shown round the enormous building where several hundred newly trained young people, seated in front of modern and expensive German computers, were doing their best to collate data for many thousands of citizens who had identical names, who might answer to several appellations, and who in many cases were not sufficiently literate to write their names.

Nevertheless, all this activity succeeded in impressing Western governments, if not everyone in Pakistan. Just six months after the coup the UK had condemned so strongly, that country's Department for International Development resumed a small programme of inter-governmental aid, which was gradually expanded in encouragement of the reform process. Not unnaturally, the Pakistani authorities presented this as testament to the soundness of their policies.

Much of the administration's activity, however, came to nothing. Some of the attempted changes were spectacular failures. Others proved counterproductive and, despite their seemingly enlightened rationales, were used by the military to enhance its authority rather than to devolve power to the grassroots and develop new democratic structures. Even the successes were flawed in important ways.

The NAB anti-corruption process, like that of the bureau's predecessor, came to be seen as being primarily a means of settling old scores. The NRB's introduction of a third tier of government, which made such good sense in theory, was particularly resented and resisted by provincial authorities, which lost much of their capacity to exercise patronage at the local level. This resistance, though not in itself an indictment of the idea, was reinforced by the probably well-founded belief that patronage was being exercised by the military at the centre instead, weakening the claim that the reform had been intended to enhance democracy. NADRA's programme for identity cards continues a decade on with a much-reduced scope.

The economic reforms seemed, on the face of it, to have been the most successful. Pakistan's GDP grew by an annual average rate of 6.1% over the five years up to 2005–06, achieving 8.6% growth in 2004–05. This was greatly assisted by the rescheduling after 2001 of 90% of Pakistan's very substantial debt to official creditors,[57] and by large injections of US financial support in recognition of Pakistan's contribution to the 'global war on terror', much of which was subsequently poorly accounted for. Musharraf's economic policies have, however, been criticised for doing little or nothing to redistribute the newly acquired wealth of a relatively small number of people to the many below the poverty line by failing to reform the country's taxation system, under which only around 1% of the population pays any direct tax.

When Musharraf, who had no prior experience of the practice of politics, initiated his reform programme, he severely overestimated what was politically possible, and the extent to which military organisational techniques could overcome the entrenched interests and customs threatened by his plans.

He was no doubt sincere in his wish to modernise and moderate the areas that he targeted. Certainly, such changes were badly needed. But, as swiftly became clear to close observers, the military's dominance of the reform effort brought with it the capability to use influence and coercion to win the assent of both individuals and institutions. As the reforms ran into difficulties and opposition, this capability was increasingly exercised. The more that this occurred, the greater the political and popular opposition. This process undermined much of the basis of the reform effort, and ultimately discredited much of what was achieved.

The ISI

Over the past two decades, Pakistan's intelligence agency has gained considerable notoriety. It has been widely accused of sponsoring covert operations in Kashmir, engaging in subversion and sabotage in India, meddling in politics in Pakistan, and supporting the Taliban in Afghanistan both before and after 11 September. As with most intelligence services, facts are hard to come by and allegations and denials abound. The organisation has been described variously as a state within a state, answerable only to itself, and as a controlled instrument of the army, from whose ranks its personnel are drawn (though it is theoretically answerable to the prime minister).

While it is, therefore, impossible to be definitive about the ISI's activities, there is sufficient literature and circumstantial evidence on which to base some observations. One certainty is that the organisation's role, status and influence have changed over time.

The ISI was originally set up in 1948 as an intelligence agency with tasks that included analysing external threats, liaising with foreign counterparts, and occasionally conducting operations. It joined an existing structure of intelligence services in which Military Intelligence provided support for military activities and the civilian Intelligence Branch dealt with non-military matters. The ISI was created to correct the shortcomings in intelligence coordination revealed during the 1947 war with India. It was brought into the political realm in 1958, during the period of martial law under General Ayub Khan, when it assumed primacy over the other two agencies.[58] In 1970, in the run-up to elections under General Yahya Khan, the ISI became yet more involved in politics at the general's instigation, and began to cultivate religious parties such as the JI to counter the influence of the mainstream parties in each of the two wings of Pakistan, notably the PPP and the National Awami League. The ascent of General Zia in the late 1970s, who further promoted the religious parties, increased the organisation's influence even more. All this was viewed askance by senior military officers, who held the traditional view that intelligence should be policy-neutral.[59] Indeed, the ISI was commonly regarded as a backwater by professional army officers, many of whom were reluctant to serve in it. Those required to do so often sought early rotation in order to escape being stigmatised by their peers, who tended to shun intelligence officers even socially.[60]

Like so many troubling aspects of Pakistan's life, the transformation of the ISI intensified following the Soviet invasion of Afghanistan. When the Soviets occupied Kabul, the ISI established connections with the Saudi government and other actors in that country that led to massive transfers of funds to Pakistan through private banks such as the Bank for Commerce and Credit International, as well as networks based on *hawala*, an informal, honour-based system for transferring funds. Among the favoured clients of both the ISI and the Saudi government during the 1980s was mujahadeen leader and warlord Gulbuddin Hekmatyar.

Following US National Security Advisor Zbigniew Brzezinski's visit to the region in February 1980, a close relationship developed between CIA Director William Casey and Director General of the ISI General Akhtar Abdur Rahman. The CIA went on to channel at least $200m to the ISI annually through its Afghan bureau, and the US funds were matched by the Saudis.[61] These arrangements had the effect of reducing the influence over Afghan affairs of both Pakistan's conventional army and its foreign ministry: the ISI had virtually a free hand.

In the late 1980s, General Rahman's successor, Lieutenant-General Hamid Gul, expanded the ISI's political role yet further by helping to create the IJI coalition, of which the PML(N) was the key member, as a counterweight to the popular PPP. In the election that followed Zia's death in 1988, the IJI came a close second to the PPP. Once in power, Benazir Bhutto, who complained that Gul was abusing his office, tried – unsuccessfully – to impose some checks and balances on the ISI.[62] Some authoritative commentators maintain that both Bhutto's brothers were murdered by the ISI, Shah Nawaz in 1985 and Murtaza in 1996.[63]

It was shortly after the 1988 election that the ISI began fomenting insurgency in Kashmir. When he replaced the deposed Bhutto in 1990, Nawaz Sharif too attempted to exercise some control over the organisation. In 1992, without consulting the army command and against their wishes, Sharif replaced Gul with radical Muslim Lieutenant-General Javed Nasir, who had no prior intelligence experience. The appointment was severely damaging, both to the ISI and to Pakistan. Nasir sought ways to support Islamist and other extremist causes around the world during his short tenure, including in Bosnia and Myanmar, reportedly even setting up a gun-running operation for Tamil militants. His activities prompted the US to challenge Pakistan's chief of army staff on the issue, who had Nasir replaced in 1993. Upon succeeding him, Lieutenant-General Javed Qazi reported that officers at ISI headquarters had taken to wearing beards, dressing in the traditional civilian dress known as shalwar kameez and absenting themselves from duty for long periods in order to attend prayers. Qazi quickly restored standard military practice and weeded out extremist elements. Qazi, who had been Benazir Bhutto's favoured choice to lead the ISI, was careful to emphasise in subsequent interviews that the ISI had not engaged in any political interference in the 1993 elections that led to Bhutto's second term of office.[64]

Meanwhile, the ISI had maintained its links in Afghanistan. When the Taliban emerged in 1994, the ISI acted as intermediary between the group and Bhutto's Interior Minister General Babar and facilitated the subsequent collaboration. Its objective was to secure a client regime in Afghanistan that was both Pashtun-dominated and pro-Islamabad. Taliban ranks were swelled by recruits from refugee camps and madrasas in Pakistan and the ISI did what it could to provide training and other support. Within two years, the Taliban had either defeated or dominated Afghanistan's other warlords. It was during this period of Taliban dominance and ISI support that Osama bin Laden began to prepare al-Qaeda for global jihad, which raises questions about the degree of complicity of the ISI with bin Laden. Whatever the truth on this point, it is clear that, as it became increasingly evident that the Taliban were running out of control, the ISI invested more in infiltrating agents into Mullah Omar's inner circle and attempting to influence him. But with the Taliban remaining laws unto themselves and impervious to Pakistani attempts to moderate their excesses,[65] Pakistan's – and the ISI's – ambition for a client regime in Afghanistan remained clearly unfulfilled.

Then, in September 2001, al-Qaeda's attacks on the United States led to an entirely new relationship between Pakistan and the US, and to a new, albeit not entirely transformed, role for the ISI.

CHAPTER TWO

Pakistan After 9/11

Uncertain allegiances

On 11 September 2001, ISI Director General Lieutenant-General Mahmood Ahmed, who happened to be visiting Washington, was given an ultimatum by the US government to declare where Pakistan stood. Musharraf, who had 'war-gamed' the possibility of having the US as an adversary, immediately came up with the only possible response: to join the coalition in the so-called 'global war on terror'. He declared this to be in Pakistan's national interest. The alternative, he wrote later, was to destroy the country for the Taliban.[1]

Despite the doubts of some corps commanders, it is difficult to imagine this decision having been otherwise. But it transformed the West's behaviour and policies towards Musharraf's regime. Although the original condemnation of Musharraf had softened as he had begun to convince Western sceptics of his benign intentions, his regime had remained a target of criticism for its absence of democracy and surplus of human-rights abuses. Now, however, Pakistan became an essential facilitating partner for the UN-sanctioned[2] military operation in Afghanistan that commenced in October 2001. Having previously received meagre financial encouragement for a somewhat doubtful process of reform, Pakistan was now showered with various forms of assistance, most though not all of them military-related, as well as being sold Western weapons systems that had no relevance to operations in Afghanistan.[3]

American and British warships lying off Pakistan's coast launched aircraft and missiles over Pakistani airspace into Afghanistan. US military forces made use of Pakistani territory and bases for purposes that went beyond what was stated in public.[4] The 'hammer and anvil' concept that formed the basis of the US strategy in eastern Afghanistan was based on the idea that US forces would harry (or 'hammer') al-Qaeda and the Taliban in Afghanistan, who would then flee eastwards, it was hoped, only to come up hard against a Pakistani army anvil in the tribal areas of Pakistan.

Pakistani intelligence helped with military targeting and in cultivating sources of influence within Afghanistan. Over the previous decade or so, US and other Western contact with the ISI, viewed askance for its support for the Taliban and Kashmiri militants, had been distant and limited. After 11 September, the US and its allies, eager to tap into every available source of knowledge about militants in any part of the world, were drawn to the ISI's considerable expertise in the field. Musharraf ensured that at least some information was passed on and that some terrorists were arrested or killed. But Pakistani expertise was not limited to names of militants and their organisations. It extended, through long and often bitter experience, to a deep understanding of the political power play among regional groups and the many and various factions within them.

Drawing on this experience, Musharraf advised his new Western allies that they should establish a presence in all the main cities of Afghanistan and not simply focus on Kabul since, though officially the capital, the city was only one of several power centres. But the Coalition was unwilling to make the heavy investment that would have been needed to follow this advice. And other commitments, in Iraq, were looming. Thus, while its main operations against al-Qaeda continued in the east of the country, the Coalition dedicated its small additional ground force to trying to stabilise Kabul. Consistent with this centralised approach, the US and its allies concentrated their political efforts on the task of establishing a central government. The Bonn Conference's selection in December 2001 of a Pashtun, Hamid Karzai, as interim president was endorsed by a *loya jirga* (grand council), and he was elected president three years later. The Coalition's unwillingness to establish a presence beyond Kabul was to persist for some years.

As the West's Afghan policy moved abruptly from aloofness to intensive engagement from 2001, it found itself suffering from the lack of experts on the ground since the severing of links in the 1990s. It was to prove exceptionally difficult for Western governments to distinguish real experts from false friends in Afghanistan after 2001, and to establish sound factual bases for decision-making. Many millions of dollars were wasted in fruitless efforts to buy the support of Afghans who were willing, at most, to be hired.[5]

Meanwhile, once the Afghan campaign had begun, Western journalists were paying the owner of the Marriott Hotel in Islamabad $500 an hour for the use of his roof from which to transmit breathless television reports against the appropriately dramatic craggy backdrop of the Margalla Hills. Some journalists ventured further into Pakistan, to places such as the Baluchistan city of Quetta, where reporters suggested that rocks thrown at television cameramen showed that the region was in anarchy, and that burning tyres signified that the whole country was in flames. Not for the last time, some Western pundits declared that Pakistan was on the brink of collapse.

In contrast to these overdrawn reports, however, the public reaction in Pakistan to the Afghan campaign was generally muted. Street demonstrations soon fizzled out. In the months before the campaign began, a number of Pakistani commentators had been saying that the government's policy towards the Taliban was both misguided and unsustainable, and many Pakistanis were deeply uncomfortable about the activity of violent militant groups in Kashmir and elsewhere. Despite deep misgivings about the US bombing campaign in Afghanistan, there was also within Pakistan much satisfaction at the prospect that these elements might now be reined in.

Musharraf made some significant changes among senior army officers in 2001. His sacking in early October of the director general of the ISI, thought to oppose Pakistan's new policy, suggested that he was prepared to take uncomfortable decisions, difficult not least because Mahmood Ahmed had played an instrumental role in his coup two years earlier. In August, under pressure from the US and the UK, Musharraf had banned a number of militant groups, including Lashkar-e-Jhangvi and Sipah-e-Mohammed, which had been involved in sectarian violence.

But Musharraf could not bring himself to break with the Taliban immediately. Diplomatic relations were maintained until the regime fell in November through a Taliban ambassador-cleric based in Islamabad. This 'representative of the Afghan government' made full use of the curiosity of the world's press to spread the word that the Taliban would never give up al-Qaeda. Only once it was clear that the regime the former 'ambassador' purported to represent had collapsed was he refused asylum in Pakistan and dispatched to Guantanamo Bay.

In both Afghanistan and Pakistan, Coalition activity became associated predominantly with military operations: the use of 'daisycutter' bombs and, notwithstanding the elimination of many al-Qaeda militants, the unsuccessful search for Osama bin Laden and Mullah Omar. The inevitable civilian losses that accompanied these operations were not, in the eyes of ordinary Pakistanis and Afghans, in any way offset by Coalition efforts to improve the lives of citizens through development and other projects.

Decades of Pakistani involvement in Afghanistan have left deep wounds. The relationship between Karzai and Musharraf was famously prickly. Zardari, who has a much better personal relationship with the Afghan president, has been assiduous in trying to change Afghan perceptions of Pakistan, and invited Karzai to attend his presidential inauguration. But opinion polls conducted in Afghanistan in early 2009 suggest that Pakistan remains deeply unpopular there, and is felt to have a negative influence in the country.[6]

In December 2001, the attack on the Indian parliament focused attention again on Pakistan's suspected links to groups committing acts of terrorism in Kashmir and India. Indian public opinion was already wounded and angry following an attack in October on the state assembly in Srinagar, the capital of Jammu and Kashmir. But the violation of the seat of the world's largest democracy, with all the political symbolism that entailed, provoked particular outrage. The Indian government placed the blame on Pakistan, moved aircraft and troops to the west, mobilised India's massive army, and deployed nuclear-capable missiles in eastern Punjab.[7] Many Indians advocated a vigorous and forceful response. The Pakistani establishment seemed surprised by this reaction, dismissing it as histrionics intended to ensure US pressure on Pakistan in India's favour. But this was a serious misjudgement of the genuine strength of feeling in India. Many in the Indian Army, in particular, were eager to avenge what they saw as the effrontery of Pakistan's

Kargil adventure in 1999 and the humiliation it caused. One Indian general was relieved of his command for being overly aggressive on Pakistan's southeastern border.

Pakistan mobilised its army as well, and for ten months the two nuclear-armed countries were on a knife edge. The region had become a nuclear flashpoint. Judging that any conflict could escalate and that the risk of the use of nuclear weapons could not be dismissed, several Western governments issued travel advisories recommending that their citizens leave both India and Pakistan. A terrorist attack on an Indian army camp in May 2002 brought the tension between the two countries to a level higher than at any time since 1971. The crisis finally eased in October, following concerted and closely coordinated shuttle diplomacy by senior envoys from the UK and US.[8] A crucial step in this process had been a visit to India in June from US Deputy Secretary of State Richard Armitage, who brought with him a pledge from Musharraf that cross-border infiltration of militants from Pakistan would 'visibly and permanently' cease.[9] India was gratified by this admission of Pakistan's prior involvements. Armitage, however, thought better of conveying the proviso that Musharraf had attached to the pledge, namely that its fulfilment was conditional on India making progress in resolving its differences with Pakistan over Kashmir, a condition that India would no doubt have found impossible to accept.

In response to the urgings of the US and the UK (in particular of Prime Minister Tony Blair) to recognise the depth of Indian feeling about the attack on the country's parliament, Musharraf did make some apparent adjustments earlier in the crisis. In January 2002, he delivered an important televised speech in which he announced bans on the militant groups Lashkar-e-Tayiba and Jaysh-e-Mohammad, which had been implicated in the attack.[10] He also urged Pakistani militants to refrain from 'lesser jihad', involving violence against others, and focus instead on 'greater jihad', or self-improvement. Meanwhile, however, terrorism within Pakistan itself both increased in frequency and widened in scope. Among the more spectacular attacks of 2002 were a suicide bomb detonated during a Sunday Christian church service in Islamabad's diplomatic enclave in March that killed and wounded several Western worshippers and a number of Pakistanis, and a car bomb outside a hotel in Karachi in May that killed 11 French engineers.

Despite Musharraf's positive steps, concerns soon re-emerged that he and the ISI, even under the leadership of the more conciliatory Lieutenant-General Ehsan ul Haq, were playing a double game, or at least hedging their bets. Banned groups reformed under other names. Arrests were followed by releases. Training camps for militant fighters in Pakistan-administered Kashmir, the existence of which were open secrets, moved to new locations. Denials of continuing involvement with militants were undermined by belligerent public declarations by senior retired ISI officers. In Musharraf's eyes, as is clear from the account of the Kargil operation in his autobiography, the 'freedom fighters' were a potential military asset.[11] If, as seemed quite possible in 2002, India were to conduct an offensive, Pakistan needed every possible resource at its disposal to defend itself.

Suspicions therefore persisted that former or lower-level ISI operatives were maintaining their networks, and that Musharraf had merely put the relationship with militant groups onto a back burner, with a pilot light that could be turned up at a moment's notice. In May 2002, just four months after Musharraf's speech banning certain militant groups and distancing Pakistan from violent jihad, US Secretary of State Colin Powell publicly accused Pakistan of continuing infiltration across the Line of Control in Kashmir.[12]

In addition, the US could obtain no clarity about how Pakistan was spending the funds it was supplied in support of *Operation Enduring Freedom* in Afghanistan. Speaking after he had retired from government service, Bruce Riedel, who had dealt with Pakistan at a high level from within the US National Security Council for many years, gave voice to the US's persistent frustration. In an interview in December 2008, Riedel accused Musharraf of 'double-dealing' for six years and of fleecing Washington for billions of dollars.[13]

As he hedged his bets internationally, the longer Musharraf was in office, the more he had to manoeuvre to preserve his position domestically. He maintained the essential support of the army by carefully selecting corps commanders and, crucially, nominating loyalists to head the ISI. He also considerably increased the allocation of profitable jobs in the civil sector to serving and retired senior officers, and expanded the granting of land to retired service personnel.

At the end of April 2002, advised that he would win easily, Musharraf held a referendum on extending his presidency by another five years. The vote-rigging and other manipulations that helped to produce the desired result were so obvious that Musharraf had personally to apologise for the overzealous behaviour of his supporters.[14] In national and provincial elections held in October 2002 in accordance with the deadline imposed by the Supreme Court in 2000, manipulation was again blatant.[15] The guided result gave the largest share of the vote to a newly created offshoot of the PML, the PML(Qaid-e-Azam) (PML(Q)). The group, which was led by wealthy Punjabis of dubious reputation, quickly became known as the 'King's Party' because of its support for Musharraf. The subsequent parliamentary proceedings were characterised by chaos and inactivity. The PML(Q) had chosen a Baluchi, Zafarullah Khan Jamali, as prime minister, seemingly to avoid the appearance of Punjabi dominance. But he fell out with the real strongman within the party, Chaudhry Shujaat Hussain. Finding that he had no power or authority, Jamali resigned in June 2004 and was replaced by Finance Minister Shaukat Aziz, for whom two safe parliamentary seats were quickly found.

Musharraf's machinations were dangerous to him personally and to those associated with him. While he was criticised by the US and others for not doing enough to deal with militancy, militants were trying to kill him for being too close to the US. Some estimates suggest that there were as many as nine attempts on Musharraf's life during his presidency. Two suicide-bomb attacks in December 2003 very nearly reached their targets. Six months later, the Karachi corps commander was attacked in the first assault of its kind on a senior serving officer. The following year, in June, Prime Minister Shaukat Aziz narrowly escaped a bomb that exploded close enough to kill his driver. Security continued to deteriorate from 2006 onwards, with the number of suicide bombs rising sharply to reach unprecedented numbers, from six such attacks in 2006, to 57 in 2007 and 63 in 2008.[16]

Musharraf's decline and fall

Opposition to Musharraf reached a climax in 2007, the year he needed to be re-elected president if he were to remain in power, and when parliamentary elections fell due.[17] The imminent prospect of these twin events presented a complex political challenge to those involved, both nationally and internationally. The dilemma for the Bush administration was that it judged that, despite his double-dealing over militant groups, Musharraf's leadership was needed to help in the fight against terrorism. At the same time, it also advocated elections and progress towards democracy. Yet the outcome of truly open and democratic elections seemed unlikely to deliver an effective system of governance for Pakistan or to provide sufficient support for the US military campaign. The only answer seemed to be for some kind of deal to be made between Musharraf and a potential elected leadership, the outcome of which, it was hoped, would do the least damage, either to Pakistan or to US interests. Such an alliance would, it was hoped, allow progress towards democracy to be coupled with engagement with the army and hence some reassurance about stability. Thus, as the PPP seemed likely to emerge the most popular party and – perhaps more significantly – the US and UK probably preferred Benazir Bhutto to her rival Nawaz Sharif, the American and British governments worked hard behind the scenes to overcome the intense personal animosity between Musharraf and the exiled Bhutto.

Ironically, several senior Indians, concerned about the possible consequences of Musharraf's departure, were also privately remarking that efforts should be made to keep him in office – a significant contrast to the antipathy felt a few years earlier towards the architect of Kargil.[18]

Even in the best of circumstances, such a task would have been fraught with difficulty. Musharraf had lived through the ineptitude, corruption and alleged criminalities of Benazir Bhutto's first two terms as prime minister, and had set the NAB against her and her husband from the moment he took power. He both distrusted and disliked Bhutto. The feelings were probably mutual. For Bhutto, any compromise arrangement would expose her to accusations of betraying the pro-democratic, anti-Musharraf platform on which the PPP had campaigned throughout her exile. It would involve accommodation with a military autocrat who had ridden roughshod over democracy and the constitution. And it would be seen as yet another abandonment of ostensible principles in favour of expediency. Moreover, since the deal was so clearly being arranged by the US and the UK, both Musharraf and Bhutto were vulnerable to the charge that they had allowed themselves to be manipulated by foreign powers, and had brought shame on the nation's honour. In view of all this, any agreement that might be reached before national elections appeared likely to be called into question soon after the polls, when the elected leader, given a sufficient popular mandate, could claim to be obliged by the vote to repudiate Musharraf.

Over the course of the year, events on the ground increasingly changed the balance of calculations. The chief justice of the Supreme Court, Iftikhar Muhammad Chaudhry, who had been party to the accumulation of constitutional changes initiated by Musharraf, was showing signs of increasing independence. Chaudhry had begun to challenge the legitimacy of the constitutional reforms he had previously supported, and in doing so he appeared to present a possible threat to the general's re-election. In March 2007, Musharraf suspended him, citing allegations of misconduct and nepotism. This caused uproar among Pakistan's lawyers, who took to the streets in unprecedented numbers. The violent police response to the protests was captured by television cameras. With the legal fraternity behind him, Chaudhry refused to resign, and four months later, the Supreme Court ruled that he should be reinstated.

The lawyers' militancy added an unusual and powerful new dimension to the mounting opposition to an already weakened Musharraf, since they were pillars of civil society who did not represent particular religious constituencies or political parties. But other protests had more violent consequences. In early July 2007, Pakistani special forces stormed a mosque in central Islamabad following an eight-day siege, leaving nearly 100 people dead. It was never clear how many of the dead were militants and how many hostages. A burst of suicide bombings and other attacks followed in direct response to the siege.

The security forces' evident lack of expertise in managing the threat of violence gave rise to widespread recriminations over the handling of the wave of militancy.

Musharraf's term of presidential office was due to expire in November 2007, at around the same time as the current parliament's term. But the general put himself up for re-election before the departing parliament, over which he and the 'King's Party' had considerable influence, rose. Thus, on 6 October, he was duly re-elected by massive majorities in the national and provincial assemblies.[19] The opposition parties boycotted the election, the outcome of which was rendered all the more dubious by the questionable legitimacy of the outgoing assemblies following the rigged elections of 2002. In addition, Musharraf would not allow the process to be subjected to ratification by the assemblies about to be elected. It seemed that Musharraf's third presidential term of office was to be secured in the dying months of assemblies that owed their existence to Musharraf's electoral and constitutional manipulations, and that the result would not be amenable to challenge from the assemblies that were – at least in theory – due imminently to be elected in a free and fair manner. Opposition parties and many commentators in Pakistan were outraged. It fell to the Supreme Court to rule on the constitutionality of the arrangement.

On 19 October, after years of threats of arrest and periods of speculation about a deal with Musharraf, Benazir Bhutto returned to Pakistan to be greeted by rapturous crowds numbering hundreds of thousands, as well as the bouts of violence customarily associated with major political events in Pakistan. The timing was carefully chosen: by waiting until mid October, Bhutto avoided acting as a focus for opposition to Musharraf's re-election, which might have affected the result and thus scuppered any possibility of a pragmatic alliance between her and Musharraf of the kind the US and the

UK were advocating. Though it is conceivable that a result thus influenced by her return would have worked in her favour, this would have been a risky strategy for Bhutto to adopt: at this stage, Musharraf's demise was by no means a foregone conclusion, and preserving the possibility of an accommodation with Musharraf left Bhutto with more options. The timing of her return also allowed Bhutto to assess and capitalise on the negative reactions to his election. To the extent that she was clearly more popular than Musharraf, her negotiating position was strengthened, such that she might be able to demand concessions from the general, or possibly even directly challenge his legitimacy at a later date.

By now it seemed probable that the Supreme Court would invalidate Musharraf's re-election. Musharraf appeared to lose his nerve and overreact. On 3 November, he took the drastic step of declaring a state of emergency, ostensibly because of the high levels of violence in the country. This came close to imposing martial law, and was a step that the US government and others had strongly advised against. It met with widespread condemnation, including from Bhutto, who rushed back to Pakistan from a brief stay in Dubai.[20] In the following weeks, thousands of Musharraf's opponents were arrested or confined to their homes, including, once again, the chief justice, as well as Bhutto and other political leaders. Imprisonment of journalists accompanied a press crackdown. New appointments were made to the Supreme Court, which then compliantly ratified Musharraf's election. Having secured his re-election, on 28 November, Musharraf relinquished the position of chief of army staff, as he had publicly pledged to do two months earlier, and was sworn in as president the next day. The state of emergency was lifted a fortnight later, though there had been little, if any, reduction in the violence it had officially been intended to quell: it had, seemingly, fulfilled its real purpose.

Meanwhile, Nawaz Sharif detected new political openings. In exile in Saudi Arabia following Musharraf's coup, Sharif had allegedly agreed to remain out of the country for ten years. He nonetheless tried to return in September 2007, declaring that he would stand against Musharraf in the presidential elections. On that occasion, he was arrested and politely but firmly put on a plane out.[21] His return on 26 November to a rather different political scene was not impeded, no doubt because Musharraf no longer felt sufficiently secure to deal with any resulting outcry. Like Bhutto, he was greeted by massive crowds.

The stage therefore seemed to be set for a fierce battle in the election due to take place on 8 January 2008. Bhutto and Sharif were not themselves eligible to stand, as one of Musharraf's many ordinances, intended precisely to block such a possibility, prohibited more than two prime ministerial terms.[22] But being back in the country meant that they were better able to mobilise and motivate their candidates, though Sharif's slightly later return put him at some disadvantage in this respect.

Bhutto's assassination on 27 December was a major shock. During her years of exile, it had become apparent that the cohesion of the PPP, founded by her father Zulfikar, was dependent upon the dynastic line: potential rivals stood no chance of taking over the leadership so long as there was a Bhutto name, and without a Bhutto, it would be uncertain what the party stood for. Her death also brought an abrupt end to the US and UK negotiations for a pragmatic arrangement between her and Musharraf. All bets about Musharraf's future were off. The only way in which the general could survive amid the political turmoil that surrounded him was with the consent of a directly elected head of government. Even if Bhutto had lived, it was never entirely clear that she would have given or maintained this consent. But now that she was gone, there was no-one with whom such an agreement would have been possible, quite apart from the fact that public opinion was disapproving of such manipulations by foreigners in any case.

In the elections, which were postponed until February, the PML(Q), the 'King's Party', was routed. The PPP, now under the leadership of Bhutto's widower Zardari, won the largest share of the vote. Sharif's PML(N) came next. After a period of haggling, and to the jubilation of many Pakistanis, Zardari and Sharif agreed that their parties should join in a coalition government.

But this jubilation, which was founded on the hope that old political and personal animosities would be subordinated to the clear need to tackle the country's many challenges, was short-lived. Once in office, the two factions were able to agree on very little, and political infighting and manoeuvring for position meant that important decisions were left unmade and the economy neglected. In early August, Musharraf finally reached the end of the line, as the two parties came together to demand his impeachment. The general announced his resignation on 18 August 2008, declaring that the charges against him were false but that he was stepping down for the sake of his nation. Having achieved his objective of ousting the man who had supplanted him, Sharif then promptly pulled his party out of the coalition.

Zardari quickly consolidated his position. Possibly as part of the deal-making between Musharraf and Bhutto, the various cases against him had been dropped in March 2008, a move he claimed as an exoneration from what he alleged were politically motivated smears. In September, he won an overwhelming majority of votes in the national and provincial assemblies, which accordingly elected him president. It was clear that this outcome had at least the tacit support of the US.[23] Musharraf, it seems fair to assume, must have been incensed for this to have been his inheritance. And, it appeared, Sharif had been outmanoeuvred.

Zardari takes the reins

In accordance with her wishes, the PPP elected Zardari as party chairman on Benazir Bhutto's death. But he demurred, nominating instead his 19-year-old son Bilawal, who carried the Bhutto family name, and accepting the post of co-chair.[24] Zardari's power over the little-known PPP prime minister, Yousaf Raza Gilani, was immediately apparent. It also soon became clear that Zardari was in no hurry to repeal the various measures Musharraf had introduced effectively to transform Pakistan's system of governance into a presidential one. Nor would he run the risk of having the cases against him reopened.

In March 2008, as one of the conditions of Sharif's membership of the governing coalition, Zardari and Sharif had reached the Bhurban Accord, under which all the judges whom Musharraf had dismissed the previous November would be reinstated. It was Zardari's subsequent failure to push the necessary statute through parliament that was the main apparent reason for Sharif's withdrawal of his party from the coalition. Many of the dismissed judges were in fact later reinstated. But Zardari would not accede to Sharif's demand that Chief Justice Chaudhry be reinstated, saying that there was no need to get caught up in the issue of specific personalities.[25] Such is the nature of the political scene in Pakistan that this disagreement prompted speculation about each side's motives. Zardari was suspected of trying to avert the risk that Chaudhry would reopen the issue of corruption charges against him, while Sharif was thought to favour precisely this outcome, which could be politically advantageous to him. (With the lawyers' protests that had begun in 2007 continuing in 2008 and 2009, Chaudhry was ultimately reinstated in March 2009, as a direct result of the lawyers' movement and allied pressure from Sharif. With his reinstatement comes the possibility that the chief justice will open cases on allegations against both Musharraf and Zardari.)

But the disagreements between the two party leaders went beyond the issue of the judiciary. In May 2006, Sharif and Bhutto had agreed on a 'Charter of Democracy', which called for the repeal of a constitutional amendment introduced by Musharraf that enhanced the president's authority in various ways, including by reinstating the president's power to dismiss the prime minister.[26] Zardari too had agreed to this, and it figured in his party's manifesto. Sharif insisted that the commitment be honoured. But Zardari temporised, maintaining that such matters should be for parliament to decide in due course. As long as Zardari's PPP remains dominant in parliament, whatever Zardari's earlier commitment, Sharif has been unable to force the issue.[27] In mid January 2009, Zardari further strengthened his position in parliament by cutting a deal with the Karachi-based MQM party, which had once strenuously battled with his late wife. When members of the MQM took up the proffered cabinet positions, which included control of the important Petroleum Ministry, the number of cabinet ministers increased by ten to the astonishing figure of 72. Such a wide distribution of responsibility has inevitably hindered the processes of government.

At the time of writing in mid 2009, Pakistani politics remained in deadlock. Despite a sharp deterioration in the security situation in early 2009, the government appeared to have little grip on events, and the opposition showed no inclination to cooperate to tackle the challenges facing the nation. Irrespective of whether or not the substance of their differences can be resolved, the personal characteristics of each of the two main party leaders suggest that cooperation would prove difficult, if not impossible. It is unfortunate that this should be so: with a thin spread of talent at senior levels of government, it is highly desirable for Pakistan to make use of whatever experience and expertise exists among its elected politicians; particularly as the country faces other chronic challenges, especially in the economic field, beyond the prevailing crisis of security.

Economic troubles

In economic terms, Pakistan was dealt a difficult hand from the start. In recent times, a five-year spurt of growth during the Musharraf years gave rise to hope, but proved unsustainable. Then, after 2006, a mixture of bad luck and bad management caused a collapse. As with so many other aspects of Pakistani life, it is instructive to examine the historical background to the current problems.

As one of the two successor states to the Raj, Pakistan received an inequitably small share of the wealth of British India. Nor has it been blessed with many natural resources. Those that it does possess, such as natural gas, coal and some minerals, have been under-exploited and require large injections of capital before they can contribute much to general prosperity. The most important resource in such a climate, water, is in desperately short supply and has been chronically mismanaged, with wasteful and poorly maintained distribution and irrigation systems, inadequate storage, and contentious arrangements for sharing. Agriculture provides employment for 44% of the population, but generates only 21% of GDP. Pakistan is now a net importer of food. The price of its agricultural exports, rice and cotton, has dropped.

Most of the country's other exports, such as textiles and chemicals, have little added value and, being subject to World Trade Organisation rules, face stiff competition from countries such as Bangladesh, China and India. In recent years, one of the few sectors to have flourished has been petroleum-fuel transportation, stimulated by the demand for fuel from NATO and US operations in Afghanistan.

The high growth rate of both the country's general population – 2.4% a year – and of its working-age population – 3% – make it even more difficult for Pakistan to sustain its 168 million people. It is, perhaps, little wonder that 74% earn less than $2 a day. Successive leaderships have had to be clever to survive when faced with these intractable challenges, and where some have failed, others have been more successful. At critical moments in its history, Pakistan has made good use of the interests of other countries to keep itself going. It is perhaps ironic that external aid has tended to be greatest during periods of military rule: under Ayub Khan in the era of regional treaties; under Zia-ul-Haq during the Soviet occupation of Afghanistan; under Musharraf after 11 September. At times when the West's interest has waned, Pakistan has relied more on other benefactors, such as China, which has helped Islamabad to develop nuclear weaponry and built strategic highways, and Saudi Arabia and the Gulf states, whose help has often included the development of the religious schools that have frequently proved to be militant breeding grounds.[28]

The impressive growth rates that Musharraf and his finance and then prime minister, Shaukat Aziz, presided over between 2001 and 2006 were widely welcomed, and some of the economic policies that helped to create them merited the international congratulations they received. Foreign investment and remittances soared as the Pakistani 'brand' gained respectability in this period. But the burst of growth was not the result of Pakistan's unaided efforts. The debt relief and massive debt rescheduling that followed Musharraf's decision to join the 'war on terror' immediately stemmed the previous haemorrhaging of reserves caused by debt repayments. Also in this period, the US provided around $10 billion in aid, the great majority of it for military-related purposes. But the situation was inherently fragile. As soon became apparent, external capital flows can be volatile. Consumption of gas and electricity soared during the Musharraf years. But no new power stations were built to meet the increased demand. The growth in imports arising from the economic expansion was not matched by increased exports. Finally, the failure to widen the tax base beyond the 1% of the population already paying income tax, in spite of the substantial profits accruing to those who had most benefited from the recent economic expansion, also limited the benefits of growth.

But the most important roots of the subsequent economic decline lay in the failure to strengthen the institutions of the state and the emergence of a national security crisis in 2007–08. The problems started in early 2007 and continued well into 2008, after the February elections and the formation of the new government. Preoccupied with political challenges, successive leaderships had little time to devote to prudent economic management. There were no fewer than five finance ministers in the space of a year. All this coincided, as bad luck would have it, with rocketing increases in the global prices of oil, food and other essential imports. Reluctant to risk popular protest by passing on these increased costs to consumers, who were in plenty of difficulty already, the government suspended the automatic mechanisms for this purpose. This left the state with an enormous bill for the resulting subsidies. The situation was aggravated by the emergence of a vigorous smuggling operation whereby heavily subsidised imported wheat was sold at much higher prices in neighbouring Afghanistan, meaning that the state was paying foreign exchange to buy the wheat and depleting its reserves to subsidise it, to no benefit of the intended recipients but to the great enrichment of some enterprising criminals.[29]

The subsidies were funded by borrowing from the State Bank of Pakistan. As a result, Pakistan's fiscal deficit grew from 4.3% in 2006–07 to a massive 7.4% in 2007–08. The global credit crunch, another unfortunate external factor, coupled with outsiders' concerns about the country's security and stability to cause foreign-exchange reserves to fall from $13.3bn in July 2007 to $3.4bn in November 2008, which represented only about one month's worth of imports. Inflation rose to 25%, the rupee depreciated by a similar amount and the stock market fell by 40% in the last six months of 2008. GDP growth in 2008 was a mere 2.3%: lower than the growth rate of the population.

More significant even than these dramatic statistics were the effects on the ground. Food was in increasingly short supply and, even before the government's financial difficulties prompted it to start reducing the subsidies in 2008, prices were rising steeply. The swingeing increases in electricity charges that came as a result of cuts in subsidies were not accompanied by improvements in the service, and by the end of 2008, there were widespread street demonstrations in protest at power cuts that often lasted for six hours a day.

Though aware of the dire economic situation, initially Zardari did not fully appreciate the magnitude of the challenge. At least $5bn was needed within months of his September 2008 inauguration if Pakistan was not to default on debt repayments about to fall due, and a similar amount would be needed soon after, over and above the payments already expected. But within hours of delivering his inaugural speech, Zardari imprudently announced that he would in no circumstances resort to borrowing from the IMF: Pakistan would simply tighten its belt.[30] That same month, he had won little sympathy and secured no new financial pledges on a highly publicised visit to Washington. Pakistan's ally China was similarly unforthcoming in October.[31] The president's visit to Saudi Arabia the following month seemed to be the last chance. At the very least, Pakistan's economic team hoped that the Saudis would agree that payments for oil imports might be deferred, as they had done in the past.[32] A traditional donor to Pakistan, Saudi Arabia had just provided $100m for earthquake relief in Baluchistan, but much more was needed. The Saudis acerbically observed that it would have helped if Pakistan had honoured earlier bilateral agreements, and declined to be immediately more helpful. Nor did the recently formed Friends of Pakistan, a group of donor countries who met in Abu Dhabi in November, offer any financial solace.

There was therefore no alternative, despite the political embarrassment, but to seek IMF support. In November 2008, a package was accordingly agreed that was heavily influenced by the sound austerity plan that Pakistan's economic team had by now put together.[33] It provided for a $7.6bn loan over a 23-month period. Pakistan would have immediate access to about $3.1bn, and the additional $4.5bn would be available subject to quarterly reviews. Such packages are never, of course, without conditions. Pakistan would have to cut spending, phase out energy subsidies, introduce tax reforms, accelerate privatisation, raise interest rates, and allow exchange-rate flexibility to correct fiscal and external imbalances and control inflation. Some of these measures were already in place, such as the elimination of subsidies on food and fuel, raised electricity tariffs, and a reduced exchange rate.[34]

IMF conditions are frequently controversial and the fund is often criticised for insisting upon measures that are 'politically unrealistic' because they might provoke protest from those affected. But this is difficult ground since, by definition, the recipient country will already be suffering economic ill-health, and remedies often involve further pain. It does, however, seem anomalous that, at a time when many central banks were easing monetary policy to stimulate economic growth, the State Bank of Pakistan increased its discount rate from 13% to 15% in fulfilment of IMF conditionality. Similarly anomalous, and in apparent contradiction of Zardari's pledge to tighten belts, was the PPP-led government's decision in mid 2008 to provide some 3.5m households with Rs2000 (around $33) every two months under the politically expedient name of the Benazir Income Support Programme, at a total cost of Rs34bn ($560m).[35]

'Talibanisation' spreads into Pakistan

As we have seen, bloodshed, violent protest and insurgencies are not new phenomena in Pakistan. The country has long experienced sectarian violence, especially in Karachi and the Northern Areas, and separatism in NWFP, Baluchistan and, to a lesser extent, Sindh, as well as murderous political and personal score-settling throughout its provinces. But the character of militant violence underwent a significant change around 2005–06 – a little over four years after the start of the US-led Coalition's operations in Afghanistan – when the frequency of suicide bombings began to increase. Until then, such attacks had been very unusual in Pakistan, with scarcely a handful each year. Then, after 2006, suicide bombings multiplied dramatically. From the middle of the decade onwards, terrorists also became demonstrably able to operate throughout the country, including in the heart of the capital, Islamabad, as shown by the defiance of the religious militants involved in the siege of the Red Mosque in July 2007, and by the attack on the Marriott Hotel close to the parliament buildings in September 2008, in which suicide bombers killed more than 50 people. In 2009, there were attacks in several towns in NWFP, Baluchistan and the FATA, and several spectacular suicide bombings in Lahore, including an attack on the Sri Lankan cricket team in March and an assault on an ISI building in May.

A number of commentators have found it convenient to describe the perpetrators of such violence as 'al-Qaeda and the Taliban'. This conveys a sense of a certain homogeneity and commonality of cause, and risks giving rise to both a belief that military action against a few key personalities would be sufficient to address the challenge, and to the positing of vague ideas for tackling the 'root causes' of protest. In reality, a wide and disparate range of actors and groupings are involved, who have complex and sometimes violently antagonistic relationships with one another.[36] While the members of these groups are mainly Pashtuns, the 'Talibanisation' of Pakistan derives its inspiration more from Sunni Deobandi militancy than from Pashtun separatism.

However, it is possible to say without oversimplification that, following a spillover of militancy in 2006 from the troubled Waziristan tribal agency into the part of NWFP known as the 'settled' area, a broadly 'neo-Taliban' movement emerged over the next year to threaten both NWFP and the FATA. This movement was distinct from the Afghan Taliban and from mainstream Pakistani religious parties such as the MMA. The groups concerned tend to reject the legitimacy of the Pakistan state and to be prepared to wage jihad on other Muslims who do not share their ideology. Just as the Afghan Taliban have links with the opium trade, the Pakistani groups are often linked to criminal and smuggling networks in transport (in the Khyber Agency) and timber (Swat). These activities, combined with killings of tribal elders, attacks on *jirgas* ('circles', or tribal assemblies), suicide bombings and other violent acts committed in the name of religion have increasingly given rise to tensions with those attached to Pashtun tribal norms.

One of the more prominent of the groups, the Tehrik-e-Taliban Pakistan (TTP), or Pakistan Taliban, was formed in December 2007 after a *jirga* decided to coordinate the activities of several groups under the leadership of a tribal militant from South Waziristan, Baitullah Mehsud.[37] The Pakistani authorities claim that Mehsud is one of the main instigators of suicide bombings in the country. At the end of 2007, the TTP captured 200 Pakistani security-force personnel and traded their release for some of its imprisoned fighters.

This new upsurge in activity engaged and stimulated other radical Sunni organisations that had been operating independently, among them the Tehrik-e-Nifaz-e-Shariat-e-Mohammadi (TNSM), centred in the Swat valley in the settled area of NWFP. Swat had formerly been a princely state and was only fully absorbed into the Pakistani state in 1969. Even after being formally incorporated, Swat had a special relationship with state authorities by virtue of its constitutional status as a Provisionally Administered Tribal Area. Among the special provisions for the region was the acceptance by Pakistan's federal authorities of a limited application of sharia law. Originally formed by local JI cadres in the early 1990s under the leadership of a veteran of the Soviet war, Sufi Mohammed, the TNSM had been weakened when hundreds of its followers were killed or detained fighting alongside the Afghan Taliban after the US-led invasion of Afghanistan in 2001. Under the operational leadership of Maulana 'Radio' Fazlullah, however, and following encouragement from the TTP in South Waziristan, the movement increased its activity in 2008–09, launching attacks on both the Pakistani state and fellow Muslims.

While the activities of the TTP and the TNSM have received most media attention, other Sunni groups active within and outside Pakistan have similarly intensified their activities and broadened their goals in recent years. In the Khyber Agency in the FATA, the Deobandi Lashkar-e-Islami under the leadership of Mangal Bagh and the Barelvi Ansar-ul-Islam run competing sharia courts and have engaged in violent sectarian conflict.

The notorious Lashkar-e-Tayiba, together with its front organisation Jamaat-ud-Dawa, was implicated in the attacks on Mumbai in November 2008. Both Lashkar-e-Tayiba and Jaish-e-Mohammed have traditionally focused on the Kashmir issue, but now operate much more broadly. Lashkar-e-Jhangvi, a Punjab-based group with much in common with Lashkar-e-Tayiba, is thought to have been responsible for the September 2008 attack on the Marriott Hotel. Lashkar-e-Jhangvi is itself an offshoot of the radical Deobandi group Sipah-e-Sahaba Pakistan, and has acted as a conduit between al-Qaeda and other Pakistani groups.

It is clear that there is a multiplicity of militant groupings and interests in Pakistan, the activity of which has markedly increased over the years following the US-led invasions of Afghanistan and Iraq. There has been a heightened focus on high-profile and Western targets, alongside a continuation of attacks on Shi'ites and other religious minorities, as well as on the Pakistani political establishment, and often violent rivalry between competing factions. This proliferation of activities and objectives presents a considerable challenge to traditional religious parties such as JI and Jamiat Ulema-e-Islam, which are in danger of being marginalised amid accusations from the newer groupings of complicity with the state at the expense of supposed religious principles.[38]

The US response

Angered by attacks on its ground forces in Afghanistan originating from the FATA, and by the apparent assistance and sanctuary afforded to Afghan Taliban fighters in South Waziristan, US forces began, possibly as early as 2002,[39] to take independent action against Pakistan's militants. The preferred instrument has been the *Hellfire* missile, launched from *Predator* and *Reaper* unmanned aerial vehicles (UAVs), or drones, operated by the CIA. The drones conduct precision attacks in Pakistani territory by tracking their targets in real time, without the need for any American 'boots on the ground'. Such attacks, which involve clear breaches of Pakistani sovereignty, were relatively infrequent during Musharraf's tenure, amounting to ten in 2006–07 according to US sources, although Pakistan claims the number is much higher.[40] But the pace was stepped up exponentially following the general's resignation in August 2008, with around 18 attacks between August and October, aimed at both medium- and high-value terrorist targets. These took place amid angry rumours, and inevitable denials, that the US had reached a secret understanding with the Pakistani authorities whereby the US would continue its drone attacks and Pakistan would issue ritual protests. Speculation focused particularly on a meeting between US and Pakistani military chiefs in August 2008 on board the aircraft carrier USS *Abraham Lincoln*.

However, the issue took on a new dimension when, on 3 September 2008, three days before Zardari was expected to be voted in as president, three US helicopters approached the town of Wana in South Waziristan. According to Pakistani reports, the helicopters landed and special forces attacked a house and killed around 20 people without, apparently, capturing any high- or medium-level militant personnel. Pakistani public opinion was outraged, and both chambers of the National Assembly voted unanimously to 'repel such attacks in the future with full force'.[41] The strategic cost of this high-risk mission in terms of increased animosity against the US may have registered in Washington, as there has not, at the time of writing, been a recurrence of such overt violation of Pakistan's territorial integrity by the US military. It cannot be assumed that, were there to be another such attack, there would not be some among Pakistan's security forces who would decide to take up arms against their country's supposed ally and partner in the fight against terrorism.

It soon became apparent, however, that the new US administration had no intention of halting the drone attacks, with the launch of a UAV strike three days after President Obama's inauguration in January 2009. American officials have claimed that at least nine of the top 20 high-value al-Qaeda targets the US identified in autumn 2008 have been killed by drones, together with dozens of lesser figures. Despite denials, it has become common belief that the US has struck a tacit bargain with Zardari and Chief of Army Staff General Ashfaq Kayani whereby the Pakistanis would quietly facilitate further drone operations while continuing to criticise them. When he visited Washington in May 2009, Zardari pressed Obama for direct Pakistani control of the drones.[42]

The use of drones remains deeply controversial, with both the violation of sovereignty involved and the impact on Pakistani public opinion problematic. A Pakistani newspaper has reported that 60 strikes between early 2006 and April 2009 killed 687 civilians and only 14 al-Qaeda leaders.[43] By May 2009, elements of Western opinion were also turning against the tactic: David Kilcullen, an influential adviser to the US military, described continuing the drone war as 'a mistake'.[44]

Pakistani action against militants

Musharraf was circumspect in his handling of the tribal regions of Pakistan, including after 2001 and his decision to aid Coalition efforts in Afghanistan. While he was quite ready to eliminate al-Qaeda operatives, he drew a distinction between these and the Afghan Taliban, and a further distinction between both groups and Pakistani insurgents. Extremism, the Pakistani army has consistently maintained, is not the same as terrorism: they call for different strategies. But pressure from the US required Musharraf to show results periodically. This he did with, for instance, a temporary clampdown on militant groups after January 2002.

In October 2007, following initial reluctance, Musharraf sent in troops to deal with disturbances in Swat, which he later cited as one of the reasons for the declaration of a state of emergency the following month. Despite heavy casualties and the displacement of tens of thousands of people, the military failed to secure a victory, and the provincial government launched a fresh peace process in April 2008. This left the field clear for Maulana Fazlullah to close several hundred girls' schools and block a successful polio-vaccination campaign, apparently on religious grounds.

Such military operations, which had no support from local populations, who deeply resented the violent intrusion into tribal areas, appeared doomed to fail. But the Pakistani army was being pressed, by the US and others, to do more to eliminate the several sources of terrorism and insurgency in the tribal regions and to bring these areas more firmly under central government control. Faced with these competing imperatives, the Pakistani authorities have in recent years cast about for non-military ways of quelling opposition and bringing stability. Under Musharraf, there were several attempts to reach settlements with local leaders and active militants in the FATA and NWFP. The idea behind these agreements was that the military would cease hostilities, and even return seized weapons, in return for a degree of cooperation. In the FATA, there were two accords in South Waziristan, in April 2004 and February 2005, and two accords in North Waziristan, in September 2006 and February 2008. Two agreements were also made in Swat, one in May 2008 as part of the peace process cited above, and another, after Musharraf's departure, in February 2009. None of the agreements succeeded.

US sources estimated that the infiltration into Afghanistan of fighters from the FATA increased by 300% following the first North Waziristan agreement.[45] Meanwhile, popular opposition to Pakistani activities to tackle militant activity both within and outside the tribal belt drew strength from allegations, which had wide support, that Pakistan was fighting 'Washington's war'.

From the February 2008 elections until well into 2009, Pakistan's national assembly, preoccupied by party-political wrangles and a serious economic crisis, appeared unable to respond to the growing challenge of militancy. The government, failing to show leadership or to craft a policy of its own on the issue, effectively handed the problem over to the army.

Thus, by mid 2008, the chairman of Pakistan's Joint Chiefs of Staff Committee was able to indicate that 112,000 troops, including the equivalent of five regular army divisions, were deployed in the FATA and adjoining areas. He claimed that 1,451 'hardcore militants' had been killed and 2,437 arrested within Pakistan, and that 'over 901 al-Qaeda operatives' had been apprehended. The toll on the security forces had also been very high: 1,112 killed and 2,770 injured by May 2008, more deaths than among all Coalition forces in Afghanistan since 2001.[46]

In August 2008, the armed forces radically stepped up their operations in the Bajaur tribal agency, using regular troops, heavy artillery and US-supplied weaponry on the ground and heavy bombing from the air by air-force F16s, supplied by the US. Following customary practice, they called on local inhabitants to hand over any armed militants and gave them notice to leave the area themselves. Around 500,000 people had to leave their homes.

According to US reports, the Pakistani military, including its elite Special Services Group (SSG), has very limited capability to operate in the FATA, and suffers frequent ambushes and attacks from snipers and improvised explosive devices. One organisation has recorded that in 122 operations between 2003 and 2008, 42 SSG soldiers were killed and 90 wounded, with another 16 killed and 29 wounded when an SSG base at Tarbela in NWFP was attacked in September 2007.[47] The army's use of non-precision weaponry and its lack of experience in counter-insurgency techniques have caused great damage to property and non-combatants, making it a target for revenge under tribal codes. This may be expected to have considerable long-term political consequences.

Following the failure of the first Swat agreement of May 2008, the government tried again with its highly controversial February 2009 ceasefire agreement. Officials agreed to the outlawed TNSM's demand for official sharia courts to be established in the Malakand division[48] of NWFP in return for a promise of peace in the region. This involved the enforcement of the Nizam-e-Adl Regulation that had been agreed in principle by both the Bhutto and Sharif governments during the 1990s. The regulation provided for the application of custom- and sharia-based law along similar lines to their application under Swat's princely ruler.

The unfortunate consequences of the agreement quickly became apparent. The TNSM's Sufi Mohammed declared that the decisions of the sharia courts would be final and not subject to appeal to Pakistan's higher courts as national law required. And the militant groups interpreted sharia with great brutality: girls' schools were burned down, people accused of crimes were flogged and beheaded and women were banned from appearing in public. Meanwhile, fighting continued despite the promise of peace. In April, soon after Zardari met Obama in Washington, Prime Minister Gilani announced the launch of a military operation to eliminate the insurgency in Swat.

By the end of May 2009, official casualty figures for the tribal regions had risen substantially. Pakistan had by this time deployed 120,000 troops along the border with Afghanistan and established 821 border posts (in contrast to the 120 or so established by the Afghan army). Civilian casualties were thought to total around 6,000. Military casualties, dead and wounded, were estimated at 5,600–6,000. In the Swat operations alone, which began in mid April 2009, military casualties were put at between 400 and 500, and terrorists killed, wounded and apprehended were said to have reached the remarkable figures of 4,000, 2,000 and 4,050 respectively, figures which are impossible to verify.[49] Some observers suggest that army losses have been considerably higher, but have been understated so as not to undermine morale.

Of possibly even greater significance than the casualty figures is the issue of the displacement of the inhabitants of the conflict-affected areas. At the end of May, the Pakistani government announced that the number of displaced persons had reached 3.4m, 2.8m of these from the Malakand division.[50] Later, the UN Office for Humanitarian Affairs stated that the number of displaced people verified as such by the Pakistani authorities had reached 1.9m by late June,[51] though many more were believed to be dispersed around the country, lodging with relatives or others.

The nuclear issue

Following its nuclear-weapons tests in 1998, Pakistan is now estimated to possess 80–100 nuclear warheads, and is urgently expanding its capacity to produce more.[52] The possibility cannot be discounted that a period of tension like the stand-off with India of 2001–02, in which observers thought it possible that nuclear weapons might be invoked, could occur again, especially if there was another terrorist incident like that in

Mumbai in November 2008. It is believed that in normal conditions, Pakistan's nuclear warheads and delivery vehicles are kept separate. But in a time of tension in which use was considered, the hardware would need to be mated together. This could render it vulnerable to attack or theft.

The increased turbulence in Pakistan has, not unnaturally, given rise to concerns about the security of the country's nuclear arsenal. Among the scenarios that have been suggested are that nuclear warheads might fall into the hands of insurgents, and that among the several thousand Pakistanis who work in the nuclear programme, there will be some who sympathise with the insurgents or who have been infiltrated as 'sleepers', who would enable this to happen. A more extreme scenario is that the Pakistani state could unravel altogether and control of the entire nuclear capability could fall into to the hands of anti-American extremists.

Such concerns can never be entirely dismissed. But they can be put into some perspective. Worries about accidents or the unauthorised use of nuclear weapons have been expressed ever since Pakistan and India declared their capabilities.[53] Soon after the 1998 tests, the Pakistani government established a Strategic Plans Division responsible for all operational aspects of its nuclear weaponry. The division was independent of the three other service arms, and was directed by Lieutenant-General Khalid Kidwai, who remained in post into 2009, after his retirement from the army. As Pakistan, like other countries, has an interest in allaying fears over nuclear safety, Kidwai worked hard to brief interested parties, including governments and international think tanks and media, about the security arrangements the division had put in place. These included a 'personality reliability programme' for the screening of personnel working on the nuclear programme; 'permissive action links' (devices to protect weapons from unauthorised detonation); and security intelligence arrangements for the Atomic Energy Commission separate from those of other state agencies. It has also recently emerged that the US government had for some time been mentoring the Pakistani authorities about nuclear-safety issues, largely in secret, at a cost of almost $100m.[54]

The US government has been careful not to dismiss the risks surrounding Pakistan's weapons. But officials have also countered some of the more extreme assertions that have gained currency in the US. In May 2009, Admiral Mike Mullen, the chairman of the US Joint Chiefs of Staff Committee, confessed to grave concern about Taliban advances in Pakistan, but declared that he was 'comfortable' about the security of nuclear weapons.[55]

Distinct from this is the issue of possible nuclear proliferation from Pakistan. The development of the Pakistani bomb owes much to the activities of A.Q. Khan, known (not very accurately) and revered in Pakistan as 'the father of the Bomb'. Notable among Khan's activities was the theft in the 1970s of blueprints for a uranium centrifuge belonging to the Urenco consortium. Benefiting also from cooperation with China on nuclear know-how and with North Korea on missile technology, Pakistan was able to keep up with India's indigenously developed programme. When evidence emerged of plans for an unauthorised visit to Iran, Musharraf ordered A.Q. Khan's dismissal from his position at the head of Khan Research Laboratories in March 2001. Following revelations of his onward proliferation, Khan was put under house arrest in 2004.[56] But just as the architect of India's nuclear programme, Abdul Kalam, became the country's president, so A.Q. Khan is regarded as a national hero in Pakistan, and Pakistan's nuclear capability is a matter for patriotic pride. Musharraf refused to allow the US to question Khan directly or to subject him to sanction beyond house arrest, and it was implausibly claimed that

Pakistani authorities had not been aware of, let alone authorised or commissioned, his proliferation activities.

Nevertheless, it can be expected that a sufficiently close
watch is now kept on Khan that it would be difficult for him to
step out of line. But to a great extent, the damage has already
been done: though Libya's programme has been shut down,
the enrichment technology Khan sold to Iran and North Korea
furnished much of the technology that formed the basis for
those countries' nuclear programmes. And no one knows who
else might have received copies of the nuclear-weapons design
he sold to Libya.

CHAPTER THREE

Internal Conflicts

As we have seen, Pakistan has had difficulty in forging a national identity ever since its inception, with ethnic and regional identities proving powerful countervailing forces. Two tribal minority groups have been especially significant. These are the Pashtuns, who predominate in the FATA, NWFP and northern Baluchistan, and the Baluchis, who have a long history of separatist protest and insurrection. Both groups are directly relevant to any effort to increase the country's stability.

The tribal regions

Many foreign commentaries about Pakistan since 2001 have criticised the Pakistani authorities' failure to control the FATA and the tribal belt in general. Such criticism has often been accompanied by assertions that this failure demonstrates that the Pakistani government cannot be a serious partner in the opposition to global terrorism. But that line of argument is weak at best. It implies that the tribal areas would be amenable to control and pacification if only there were sufficient political will. In practice, control of the FATA is probably impossible within the sort of timescale envisaged by those who impatiently advocate it. If it were to come about, it would be likely to require a generation or more of effort, rather than a year or two. In any case, Pakistan's objectives in dealing with militancy in the tribal regions and in Afghanistan have never been the same as those of the US. Pakistan's main aim has been to secure its own stability and to protect its interests vis-à-vis India.

Most of the population along or near the border with Afghanistan is tribal. Pashtun tribes inhabit the northern part of the region, and Baluchi tribes the southern part, with tribes in both areas divided into sub-tribes. Pashtuns and Baluchis alike have always strongly maintained their independence from outside authority, often defiantly opposing attempts to limit or encroach upon centuries-old socio-political structures, as well as frequently warring among themselves. Over time, the areas in which they live, collectively described here as the tribal regions or areas, have come to be subject to various external systems of governance and divided into different administrative regions. Much of the border land has never been subject to full central-government control, either under the colonial government of British India or under the Pakistani governments that succeeded it. The tribal regions have been incorporated into what is now the Pakistani state in different ways over different timescales. The constitutional position of the seven agencies and six 'frontier regions'[1] that make up the FATA is the most anomalous of the various arrangements.[2]

In the nineteenth century, the tribal belt was the front line in the 'Great Game' of strategic rivalry between Britain and Russia, which was stimulated by British concern about the threat of Russian encroachment into India. British attempts to pacify Afghanistan and the contiguous region in British India included three wars, in 1838–42, 1878–81 and 1919. The British won some battles and, in the second Sikh war in 1849, defeated Sikh rulers in what is now Punjab and NWFP. But

Britain failed to prevail in Afghanistan. The third Afghan war concluded with Afghanistan's independence. This experience led the British to conclude that this inhospitable land and the fierce, unruly and religiously zealous tribes who inhabited it were best left alone to manage themselves, for better or worse, according to their customs. The British objective in the region became limited to persuading or compelling the tribes not to cause trouble on British-administered territory.

In November 1893, British administrator Sir Mortimer Durand signed an agreement with Amir Abdur Rahman Khan of Afghanistan on the border between Afghanistan and the western limits of British India. Despite all the political and military upheavals that were to follow over the next century, this border, known as the Durand Line, remains of immense political significance. The line extends 2,560 kilometres from the present NWFP in the north to the westernmost tip of Baluchistan in the south. Though most of the line follows natural features such as rivers and watersheds, it also cuts through traditional Pashtun tribal lands: this can be seen in Waziristan in particular, where it splits at least 12 villages and divides other villages from their fields.

The line has been contentious from the very beginning. Pakistan regards it as a legitimate international boundary, confirmed by treaties in 1905, 1919, 1921 and 1930. Afghanistan and many Pashtuns in the region reject it as an arbitrary division of the Pashtun heartland. Afghanistan formally repudiated any formal status for the line in a *loya jirga*, or grand national assembly, in 1949. It continues to reject any suggestion that it should alter its long-standing view that the line has no legal validity, and some Baluch nationalist groups regard the Durand Line Agreement as illegal, and therefore null and void from the start.[3] The strength of the differences over the Durand Line have cause some commentators to view the line as central to the current problems in Afghanistan and Pakistan, and others to suggest that resolution of the issue is necessary in order for these problems to be solved. But the line's unresolved status has in many ways suited both sides. It has enabled Afghans to maintain their dream of the future incorporation of Pakistan's tribal areas into Afghanistan and eventual access to the sea. And, for all Pakistan's protestations and expressions of concern about instability, the maintenance of a Pashtun tribal belt gives that country greater scope to influence events in Afghanistan, all the more important to it if the US-led Coalition were to pull out. It is worth noting that Pakistan never tried to secure formal recognition of the line as part of the 1988 agreement that ended the Soviet occupation, nor did it ask the Afghan Taliban regime to recognise it: certain strategic considerations, it seemed, took precedence over the disadvantages of the status quo.[4]

It was in 1901, under British rule, that the tribal agencies were first formally designated as such. This was as part of arrangements for the administrative separation of the Pashtun region from the Province of Punjab, under which the Pashtun region was to be divided into 'tribal agencies' and 'settled districts'. The latter became the separate province of NWFP. Initially five in number, the tribal agencies were not subject to taxation by the colonial power. They did not come under the administrative purview of NWFP, but were administered by 'political agents' under the orders of the governor of NWFP, who was himself directly responsible to the viceroy of India. It was expressly stipulated that the governor was not to interfere in the internal affairs of the tribes, but that it was among his duties to keep in close contact with them and, so far as possible, maintain friendly relations. The governor was also responsible, through the political agents, for disbursing the tribal allowances that had been agreed by a series of treaties with tribal leaders, seeing that the tribes fulfilled their treaty responsibilities, and advising the viceroy on tribal affairs. A Frontier Crimes Regulation, which was consolidated from earlier versions in 1901, governed the dispensation of justice in the agencies, and was enforced by means of *jirga*. The regulation was intended to reflect local customary, rather than British, law. Control was maintained by tribal leaders and their constabulary forces. On the occasions when these arrangements and the agreed financial inducements proved insufficient to prevent trouble, the British would mount punitive expeditions, impose collective fines or other retribution, and then withdraw speedily. This system of control came to be known as 'burn and scuttle'.[5] It is hardly surprising that, rather than encouraging tribal people to cooperate with the central authorities, it sowed the seeds of Pashtun independence movements.

Thirty years after the creation of the agencies, the British conducted an enquiry into the situation in the tribal regions. It found that there remained a strong feeling of separateness from the rest of India among Pashtuns, including those in the settled area of NWFP. The Simon Commission, which sat from 1928 to 1930, recorded the view of tribal leaders in Peshawar that:

> The contiguity of the province ... with independent territory and Afghanistan, the free intercourse between the people on both sides of the border line, the simplicity of their ideals, customs, and mode of life, and especially their descent from common stock, strongly distinguish the people of our province from those of the rest of India.

In the light of such attitudes, the Simon Commission concluded that 'British India stops at the boundary of the administered area'. The boundary referred to was that between the tribal regions and the rest of British India.[6]

Upon Indian independence and the partition of British India into India and Pakistan, the tribal belt remained anomalous. The arrangements for the governance of the regions of what had been British India once Britain gave up its authority varied according to the status of the regional entity concerned. Britain's relations with the 500-odd princely states that were widely distributed throughout its Indian empire had been managed by a series of treaties. These treaties ceased to be valid on Britain's withdrawal from the subcontinent. Princely states, at least theoretically, had three choices: to join India, to join the newly created Pakistan, or to remain independent for a specified period until they had decided one way or the other. Provinces that had been directly administered by the British, of which NWFP was one, were dealt with by the Partition Agreement. This offered a more limited choice, which was to be made by referendum: to join India or to join Pakistan. Independence was not on offer.

Although NWFP bordered what was to become Pakistan and the great majority of its inhabitants were Muslims, the outcome of its referendum was not a foregone conclusion. Its provincial government, which was dominated by the Indian Congress Party, advocated joining India, as it believed that this would give the province greater autonomy. But just before the referendum, the Congress Party decided to boycott the vote, and instead registered its support for an independent Pashtunistan.[7] When the poll went ahead, more than 50% of those eligible to vote in the referendum registered their support for joining Pakistan.

As for the tribal agencies, their relationship with the British had, like that of the princely states, been determined by a series of treaties, in this case between British New Delhi and key tribal leaders. As the treaties lapsed, the British sponsored a *jirga* that offered the same options as those available to the

British-administered provinces: a choice between India and Pakistan. Afghanistan raised objections, which were initially supported by India. These were that the Durand Line was not a validated international boundary and that the tribes had separate agreements with the British government and therefore functioned as independent nations, meaning that they, like the princely states, should also be given the third option of independence. The Afghans may have calculated that, had the option of independence been chosen, this would have led to the creation of a Pashtunistan that might then have decided to join Afghanistan. So strong was Afghanistan's opposition to the proposed arrangement that it was the only country to oppose Pakistan's application to join the UN in 1947.

As it was, following considerable Pakistani inducements, all the tribes agreed to go with Pakistan. For its part, the newly created state was careful to avoid provoking opposition in this sensitive region. It withdrew all its regular army units in December 1947, leaving only five battalions of the locally recruited Frontier Corps to maintain order. This was in marked contrast to the approach of the British, who had maintained around 48 Indian Army battalions along their frontier with Afghanistan.[8]

It was not until 1949, two years after independence, that Pakistan negotiated an 'Instrument of Accession' with tribal leaders. This provided that the FATA would keep the semi-autonomous status and the administrative arrangements set out by the British in 1901. The agencies would be governed by Pakistan's president via the governor of NWFP. The governor's authority was to be administered in each agency by political agents, who had executive, judicial and tax-collecting roles (district deputy commissioners fulfilled these functions in the six newly created frontier regions that also formed part of the FATA). The Frontier Crimes Regulation of 1901 remained valid. In return for their quiescence, the tribal leaders would continue to receive subsidies and allowances as they had under the British.

The 'tribal areas' were subsequently defined in Pakistan's 1973 constitution, which laid out which areas and districts qualified as such and formalised the areas' special nature, broadly along the lines of earlier arrangements.[9] The constitution guarantees the basic rights of the people of Pakistan, including those in the FATA. But, while the FATA are represented in the national parliament and therefore have a role in framing legislation that applies in the rest of the country, parliament has no power to legislate for the FATA: it falls to the president to extend laws to the FATA through Presidential Regulations. The FATA have no police or law courts. Nor does the Supreme Court have any jurisdiction to safeguard and enforce constitutional rights there. This leaves the executive authority of the NWFP governor and the political agents unchecked and unquestioned. Ultimately, while the inhabitants of the FATA have rights guaranteed by the constitution, in practice, the means for upholding these rights are limited.[10]

Bordered to the west by 600km of the Durand Line, the FATA now comprise seven semi-autonomous agencies – Khyber, Mohmand, Bajaur, Kurram, Orakzai, North Waziristan and South Waziristan – and the six frontier regions, which are situated within NWFP. The FATA cover an area of 27,000km^2 inhabited by 3.5 million people, the great majority of whom belong to Pashtun tribes.[11]

Distinct from the FATA are the Provincially Administered Tribal Areas (PATA). There are seven of these in NWFP, including the troubled Malakand division, which contains the district of Swat, and five in Baluchistan. All those in NWFP are directly administered by the NWFP provincial government. Some – Chitral, Dir and Swat – remained princely states until their full incorporation into Pakistan in 1969, having joined Pakistan in 1947 but retained considerable autonomy and their princely status.

Apart from these special areas, the remainder of the provinces of NWFP and Baluchistan, where national and provincial laws apply in the same way as in the other two provinces of Pakistan, are also highly tribal, though the terrain in these regions is generally less mountainous, and parts of NWFP are exceptionally fertile.

'Pashtunwali': the Pashtun tribal code

The legendary Pashtun nationalist leader, Khan Abdul Wali Khan, who died in 2006 aged 89 having spent his life leading a movement that agitated against the British and Pakistani authorities for an independent Pashtunistan, remains a symbol of the Pashtuns' independence of spirit. In 1972, asked by a journalist about his loyalties and to whom he felt his first allegiance, he said: 'I have been a Pashtun for six thousand years, a Muslim for thirteen hundred years, and a Pakistani for twenty-five.'[12] Wali Khan was regarded almost as the embodiment of the Pashtun tribal code, or Pashtunwali, a collection of long-established ethical and customary norms of communal life. Although it has been seriously eroded in recent decades, the code's obligations remain relevant today, and have an impact on tribal attitudes towards military and other operations in Pakistan and Afghanistan.

In the early 1970s, US anthropologist and Afghanistan specialist Louis Dupree collected and summarised what he judged to be the main generally accepted features of the code. Among these were individual and collective obligations to:

- Avenge blood (*badal*). This obligation may persist over generations until it is fulfilled.

- Fight to the death for a person who has taken refuge with one, regardless of that person's lineage *(nanawati)*.
- Defend to the last any property entrusted to one *(ghayrat)*.
- Be hospitable and provide for the safety of the persons and property of guests *(melmastia, mehrmapalineh)*.
- Pardon an offence on the intercession of a woman of the offender's lineage, a *sayyid*[13] or a mullah. (An exception is made in the case of murder: only blood or blood money can erase this crime.)[14]

Running through all these are notions of honour, bravery, manliness, chivalry, steadfastness and righteousness. Historically great warriors, the Pashtun tribes maintain arsenals of arms and ammunition, *qaumi aslaha*, for use in tribal and other feuds. Every tribesman considers it his inalienable right to carry arms from childhood. Colonial accounts abound with tales of young men who gained honour by fulfilling the obligations of *badal* and wiping out enemies. At the start of the Second World War, the British estimated that nearly every tribesman who had any possessions at all owned one or more rifles of European or local manufacture, which he treasured above all else.

Dupree describes Pashtunwali as a 'tough code for tough men who, of necessity, live tough lives'. It allows little room for dissidence. If a coward returns home, his mother will disown him; if he runs away from a fight, he will not be buried with the Muslim rites but will become a ghost, never to reach Paradise.[15]

The former head of the ISI's Afghan bureau, Mohammad Yousaf, who mentored mujahadeen from 1983 to 1987, confirms the significance of Pashtunwali in tribal life, and the hardiness of its adherents: 'Even a jihad does not stop *badal*'; 'Physical courage is central to the Afghan character.' Although possessed of many of the attributes necessary for good soldiery, the effectiveness of Pashtun warriors in the fight against the Soviets was, Yousaf observed, hindered by inflexibility and a preferred mode of fighting that 'involved much shooting, the inflicting of casualties, the opportunity to show off their courage and the possibility of war booty'. Canny covert operations were not at all favoured by Pashtun fighters, even if they might prove more effective and less dangerous.[16]

Clearly such mores, even if they are not always fully observed in practice, have important implications for tribes' behaviour towards foreigners, non-Muslims, and even members of a different tribe or sub-tribe, especially if the outsider in question has taken up arms in someone's home territory. An individual or a tribe may view it as an overriding matter of pride and honour to drive out any intruder who violates the sanctity of *qaum*, or the homeland, and to kill him if he has drawn blood. Just as Soviet troops in Afghanistan in the 1980s were regarded as intruders, so are the US and other Western forces there now. Similarly, there may be an obligation to provide refuge to an individual under threat, even if he represents other interests or causes: the greater the threat to the guest, the greater the honour accruing to the host. The *nanawati* principle might, for example, be invoked in relation to Afghan Taliban or Pakistani militants who entered the FATA and other tribal regions fleeing pursuers in Afghanistan.

Pashtunwali would be an exceptional, indeed a unique, code of behaviour if it were always strictly observed. Expediency and the balancing of interests significantly qualify its application in practice. What might be viewed as hypocrisy in Western society may be interpreted locally as a pragmatic acceptance that the negative consequences of rigidly adhering to certain behavioural standards in all circumstances makes an inflexible approach to the rules impractical. As British colonial administrators and others after them discovered, and as can be discerned from the text of the Durand Line Agreement, money can also be a powerful influence on behaviour. The role of money as a means of enhancing power, respect and influence is often more significant in Pashtun culture than the wealth itself, and helps to make money a useful bargaining tool for outsiders to use in their dealings with tribal leaders. But even money has its limits. A British administrator in the 1930s suggested that for all practical purposes, the prevailing law in the tribal areas was: 'He will hold that has the power and he will take that can.'[17]

During the 1980s Afghan War, many Pakistani tribesmen had a foot in both camps: while thousands participated in the jihad against the Soviets and supported the mujahadeen, if there was a financial incentive to do so, the same people might also help the Soviets. Since, if they were antagonised, the tribes could close the supply routes depended on by both sides, they developed a sort of immunity. As a result, they were able to hire out their vehicles to the pro-Soviet Afghan army while at the same time charging mujahadeen to use the routes they controlled.[18]

Western dealings with the tribes in the aftermath of 2001, when all sorts of inducements were used in the hunt for al-Qaeda, appeared to bear out the old, cynical quip: 'You cannot buy an Afghan, you may only rent him'[19] – though the meagre return on investment might suggest that the rental charges were frequently overpriced. It seems likely that Pakistani tribesmen in the FATA profit from both sides now, just as they did in the 1980s.

Pakistani officials and military officers have regretfully observed that the tribal code is eroding, and with it the implicit notion of the reciprocity of obligations. Some commentators suggest that the code has become entirely irrelevant; others disagree. Certainly, foreign mujahadeen, from neighbouring Central Asia in particular, who have been in the region since the late 1970s and who observe different customs, have married into local tribes without always assimilating the native codes of conduct. More importantly, the centrality of the idea of jihad to the war effort in the 1979–89 Afghan War had the effect of increasing the influence of clerics in Pakistan's border regions at the expense of the maliks (tribal leaders). Thus, traditional codes in the tribal regions have to a degree been supplanted by more doctrinaire religious attitudes, with uncertain consequences for stability. And, crucially, it does seem to be the case that in many instances, reciprocal obligations embedded in Pashtunwali are no longer being honoured. In particular, the code requires that a guest or someone who has taken refuge does not behave in a manner that would cause difficulty or embarrassment to his host. In practice, Pakistani sources close to such matters have suggested that militants who have fled into the FATA from combat areas in Afghanistan have continued their fight in the tribal areas. In doing so they expose their hosts to retribution from the Pakistani authorities, other tribesmen and, increasingly, US drones. This is not to suggest that some hosts may not be complicit with their 'guests'. But some very likely had no choice in the matter.

The FATA today

Life in the tribal regions is hard. Living standards and opportunities are well below those found in the great majority of developing countries. The contrast with the conspicuous affluence of the well-to-do in Pakistan could hardly be more marked. Even those enriched by profits from the opium poppy lead simple lives. The region's generally mountainous terrain is exceptionally inhospitable. Communications infrastructure is underdeveloped. There is no industry and very few opportunities for employment. At 17.5%, the literacy rate is well below the Pakistani average of 44%; female literacy stands at a mere 3%. With one doctor for every 7,700 people, access to health care is limited even in comparison to the low standard prevailing nationally, where there is on average one doctor for 1,220 people.[20] There is little access to safe drinking water, and publicly funded education is virtually non-existent.[21] The proportion of cultivated land that is under irrigation is below half the national average, which partly accounts for a wheat yield that is only 40% of the average yield of comparable areas of farmland in the country.[22]

The system of governance and administration suffers from the shortcomings of the 1901 Frontier Crimes Regulation, which attempts to apply principles of tribal law to matters of law and order in the region. The regulation was draconian and outmoded even when it was first introduced: surrounded by controversy, it is a patent anomaly in the twenty-first century. Its provisions for detention, for example, have routinely been misused. But the regulation's deficiencies go beyond its history of abuse. The Pakistani state continues to apply its concepts of collective responsibility and collective punishment. Thus tribes, sub-tribes and clans continue to be threatened with the destruction or confiscation of property and collective fines for the misdeeds of a few.

Prime Minister Gilani, recognising that change was needed, pledged in his inaugural speech in March 2008 to abolish the Frontier Crimes Regulation.[23] However, as a Punjabi who did not know the FATA well and had not consulted those concerned, he was unaware of the strength of resistance to change that existed in many quarters in the tribal regions, and did not anticipate the likely response to what was no doubt a well-intentioned move. Faced with opposition from the leaders of two of his coalition partners in NWFP, who observed that Gilani had said nothing about what would take the place of the regulation, the prime minister swiftly watered down the pledge to envisage modification rather than abolition.

Arrangements for the political representation of the FATA at the national level are similarly outmoded. The adult franchise was only introduced in 1997. Before then, the FATA's delegates to the National Assembly were elected by maliks and elders, who make up around 1% of the population. Pakistan's Political Parties Act does not apply to the FATA, and national political parties are not permitted to campaign or be represented under their own names there. Because of this, and because of the decline in the influence of maliks and elders and the increased influence of the mullahs, FATA members of the national parliament have in recent years tended to be clerics. Additionally, as the FATA are ruled directly by the president (through the NWFP governor), they do not have an equivalent of a provincial assembly such as exists in NWFP.[24]

Where steps have been taken to give the FATA's inhabitants more say in matters that might affect them, they have proved controversial and even destabilising. At the end of 2004, Musharraf's arrangements for local representative assemblies, which had been introduced in the rest of Pakistan in 2000, were extended to the FATA, although with more restricted powers and a much smaller number of seats reserved for women. The arrangements were viewed with intense suspicion within the region, where they were thought to be an attempt to undermine traditional power structures and the role of tribal leaders. Rather than acting as a stabilising force, the changes thus contributed to mistrust and uncertainty.

Local government reforms introduced in the tribal regions of NWFP also had some unfortunate consequences. The reforms abolished the position of commissioner, the provincial governor's senior regional representative in those regions, who had been tasked with maintaining law and order and good governance, and providing a link between tribal areas and the districts they neighboured. The position of magistrate for the tribal areas was also abolished, further reducing the capacity to enforce law and order and administer disaster relief in the tribal areas. Since NWFP magistrates were part of the same bureaucratic structure as the FATA's political agents and the province's own commissioners, the abolition of the post also diminished the pool of officers eligible to reach those positions.[25]

Gilani may have also had these problems in mind when, following the opposition to the abolition of the Frontier Crimes Regulation, he established a two-person commission to investigate possible ways forward on tribal areas governance. There have, however, been similar studies in the recent past, each of which made recommendations that were not followed up.[26] At the time of writing, the commission has made no visible progress, and the original impetus from central government appears to have dissipated.

Other changes, including increased intervention in tribal affairs by federal authorities, have had more profoundly unsettling effects on the tribal areas, reducing the already limited influence of the state, as well as that of traditional tribal leaders. The military operations in Afghanistan after 2001 caused an even greater erosion of traditional power structures than did the war of the 1980s, with a further increase in the prominence of mullahs within tribal power structures.

In late 2001, the paramilitary Frontier Corps, made up of FATA tribesmen led by regular army officers, was deployed to block infiltration by al-Qaeda, Taliban and other fighters opposing the Coalition in Afghanistan. It performed poorly.

After successive defeats in skirmishes, including the surren-
der of several units apparently without a fight, doubts arose
about the allegiances of Frontier Corps soldiers. In June 2002,
the Pakistani army, which never normally operated in the
FATA, deployed a division into the Khyber and Kurram agencies. In March 2004, the army markedly increased its presence,
with search-and-destroy operations in the North and South
Waziristan agencies, meeting widespread resistance. Some
Pashtuns have described the deployment of the army into the
FATA in 2004 as the greatest policy error made in the region
since independence.[27] The emergence of a Pakistani Taliban
and the subsequent further escalation of the Pakistani military
presence were to follow.

Army officers have maintained that the central government
is constitutionally empowered to send security forces anywhere
in the country in order to quell anti-state activity.[28] But tribes-
people resented the incursions as violations of Jinnah's pledges
not to send in troops and to resolve disputes through traditional tribal methods. In the period after the 2004 deployments,
several hundred maliks were assassinated for not sufficiently
supporting, or presenting a challenge to, particular political
interests. Compounding the undermining of traditional structures were the attempts of three separate federal authorities to
exercise their influence: the political agents officially responsible for the FATA; the Frontier Corps; and the newly prominent
army. Each had its relationships with different groups and
individuals. Traditional tribal readiness to accept inducements
from several competing paymasters added to the confusion.
After 2004, army commanders, outranking the weak political
agents, came to dominate and be viewed as the government's
main representatives. But all these destabilising trends have
contributed to the emergence of yet more competing hubs of
power.

Plans for a way forward

Because of the difficulty of gaining access to these mountainous and semi-governed areas, it has fallen to the army to administer infrastructural improvements intended by Islamabad to help pacify the tribal regions. In mid 2008, the army claimed to have constructed nearly 2,000km of roads, a small number of schools and health units, and some water-supply schemes.[29] But such projects have been overshadowed by the army's use of force in the regions, and do little to repair the damage caused by warfare. Nor do they represent attempts to influence locals in the direction of long-term shifts in attitudes that might help to stabilise the FATA.

Looking at the longer term, the Pakistani government recently promulgated a FATA Sustained Development Plan, to be implemented over nine years to 2015 at a cost of $2.06bn. Pakistan would contribute $1bn and the US $750m, with the balance hoped to be made up by other international donors. The plan's aims include improving public services, increasing government capacity in the region, promoting sustainable use of natural resources, and stimulating economic activity.[30] But though the plan was endorsed by the government elected in 2008, there has been no perceptible progress on it to date.

Both the George W. Bush and the Obama administrations have wrestled with the problem of promoting stability in Pakistan's tribal regions through the provision of assistance, but with few results. In March 2009, Obama announced what he described as a 'comprehensive new strategy for Afghanistan and Pakistan', the result of a 60-day inter-agency review. Its overarching goal was 'to disrupt, dismantle and defeat al-Qaeda in Pakistan and Afghanistan and to prevent their return to either country in the future', recognising 'the fundamental connection between the future of Afghanistan and Pakistan'.[31]

Perhaps the announcement of such a strategy and its personal endorsement by the president will give it momentum and lead to the results that have hitherto proved elusive. But the document contains little that is new, and at the time of writing, much of it remains to be realised. Obama has also called on Congress to pass a bipartisan bill, sponsored by Senators John F. Kerry and Richard Lugar, which authorises $1.5bn worth of non-military support to Pakistan each year for five years, and another bipartisan bill to create 'opportunity zones' for economic development in Pakistan's border regions. Both bills have been under consideration for well over a year. The eager anticipation expressed in late 2007 by senior Pakistani officials about the opportunity zones has long since dissipated.[32]

Even if the legislation is passed, there will be profound difficulties in spending and distributing such large packages of assistance. Pakistan's absorptive capacity is severely limited at the best of times, that of the tribal regions even more so. The contribution made to the further weakening of already vulnerable traditional tribal structures by central government 'interference' over the past five years may have increased the existing determination of the tribal regions to reject government development programmes and similar measures. In this context of limited capacity and the tribes' apparent determination to maintain autonomy, and in view of the current and foreseeable security climate, progress on development is bound to be slow.

The difficulties of achieving reform in the FATA are borne out by recent polls undertaken by Pakistan-based NGOs. While dissatisfied with existing arrangements, respondents viewed the option of moving closer to the rest of Pakistan as even less desirable than the status quo. The polls indicated little popular affection for the current system of law and order as set out in the antiquated Frontier Crimes Regulation. Only

3.2% of those surveyed favoured retaining the regulation in its current form. Thirty-one per cent wanted to see it abolished, while 40% preferred amendment to abolition. But the alternative of adopting the federal justice system only had the support of 12.8%. Nearly 45% of respondents favoured sharia law and 36% would prefer the *wolasi jirga,* or tribal-assembly system.[33]

The traditional tribal system of leadership has undoubtedly been severely damaged; by the assassination of maliks and the emergence of new sources of power and influence, not least the raised profile of the mullahs, as well as by the general dislocation of war. There are now serious questions about whether it can be restored. Furthermore, there is heated debate both within the region and outside it about whether, assuming it were possible, it would even be desirable to go back to the old ways.[34]

The dilemma is stark. The old system of governance in the FATA was never truly effective: peace and stability always hung by a thread. Now, in an atmosphere of acute instability, which has been exported to other parts of Pakistan, the same system no longer exists. Even if it did still exist, or were somehow revived, there is every reason to judge that it would not prove adequate to the task. And yet it is also clear that any concerted attempts to alter the system by which the tribal regions are still officially governed, or to make serious economic or social changes, will prove exceptionally difficult. Preliminary efforts to explore the possibility of reform, undertaken by the ANP, the dominant political party in NWFP and hence the most closely connected to fellow Pashtuns in the FATA, have met with rebuffs and even, in 2008, an attempt on the life of the party's president.

But, though any innovations would need to be advanced with great care, some change is necessary. The extension of the Political Parties Act to the FATA might be less contentious than other changes, and would seem to be both equitable and overdue. It would allow mainstream parties to campaign for election in the FATA under their own names (in recent elections, some candidates did make clear that they were aligned with particular parties, but could not do so formally). It might also encourage the FATA towards greater involvement in national politics.

On other issues, opinion is more sharply divided. A crude characterisation of the distribution of views might be that non-Pashtuns who follow such matters tend to favour the integration of the FATA into the wider federation sooner rather than later, and believe that this should be achieved using a judicious mix of incentives and, if ultimately necessary, coercion. Those Pashtuns who favour such an objective in principle tend to consider that integration can only come about within a framework of generational change and would therefore prefer to proceed with great caution over an extended timescale. But many other Pashtuns, especially those who see themselves as part of a tribal tradition, reject the idea of constitutional change outright, for reasons both of principle and practicability. The principle is that it ought to be left to the tribes to decide on whether changes to how the region operates are desirable and, if so, what kinds of changes should be made, and to implement agreed changes according to traditional methods. The practical objection is that no change will be possible unless it has the support of the tribal leaders. The difficulty here is that there is no clarity or agreement about who the 'tribal leaders' now are, and where power actually lies after three decades of turmoil.

Baluchistan

The insurgency in the FATA and the increasing use of the Pakistani army there have distracted international attention from the resurgent violence in Baluchistan. The current problems in this large and sparsely populated province are of less direct relevance to *Operation Enduring Freedom* in Afghanistan than those in the FATA. However, Baluchistan hosts, among other things, an important supply line linking US and NATO operations in Afghanistan with the coast. Though in mid 2009 a significant proportion of NATO's fuel supplies reached Afghanistan by other routes, the prohibitive costs involved in developing further alternative routes meant that the majority of fuel and the great majority of heavy equipment for Afghan operations was still transported through Pakistani Baluchistan. The significance of the Baluchistan route also grew mid year, as the US increased the numbers of its troops in Afghanistan. Baluchistan's apparently intractable difficulties also have implications for the stability of Pakistan itself, as well as being of concern to several of Pakistan's neighbours. Iran and Afghanistan have an interest in developments in Baluchistan because of their sizeable Baluchi populations. Meanwhile, the potential strategic implications of China's involvement in the $2bn development of the port of Gwadar on the Arabian Sea in the far southwest of the province are of concern to both India and the US.

In addition to supply lines and a high concentration of Pakistan's most valuable natural resources, there are several other strategic and economic reasons for Pakistan and outsiders alike to take an interest in Baluchistan. The province is home to some of the country's nuclear-weapon test sites and two of its three naval ports; it is close to the strategically important Strait of Hormuz and the Gulf states; it has porous borders with Afghanistan and Iran; trafficking routes for narcotics emanating from Afghanistan run through it; it has the potential to host gas pipelines; and two of the three military bases in Pakistan used by the US military operating in Afghanistan, Pasni and Dalbandin, are stationed there.

Tribal discontent

The Baluchi tribes, like the Pashtuns, strongly value their autonomy from central authority, and have fought on numerous occasions to gain or retain it. Also like the Pashtuns, most live in chronic poverty in inhospitable terrain, subject to discrimination and sporadic violence from the central authorities, which fosters further resentment and opposition.

The tribal nature of much of Baluchistan has – in a further parallel with the FATA and NWFP – always presented central authorities with difficulties of governance. By the nineteenth century, the area inhabited by the Baluchi tribes had been carved up by a series of treaties between British India, Persia and Afghanistan. The British labelled a strip of the borderland next to Afghanistan 'British Baluchistan', but beyond this, left the Baluchis alone, so long as they did not impede British military access to Afghanistan. As with the Pashtun maliks, the British paid allowances to the *sardars*, the Baluchi tribal chiefs, to keep them from causing trouble, but otherwise maintained little contact.[35] Unlike in the Pashtun areas further north, there were no special arrangements for the governance of particular areas of Baluchistan: the region became an ordinary part of British India.

When the state of Pakistan was established, some Baluchi tribes tried to assert their autonomy by force. The first conflict in 1948 was followed by the disturbances of 1958, 1962 – when the Pakistani army significantly increased its garrisoned presence in the province – 1973–77, and 2005 to the present day. Of these, the bloodiest was that of the 1970s, with the initiation in 1973 of a brutal campaign of suppression on the orders of Zulfikar Ali Bhutto. Weaponry and helicopters were supplied by the shah of Iran, who feared that the uprising might spread among the million or so Iranian Baluchis. Some 55,000 Baluchis were pitted against 70,000 Pakistani security personnel, leading to the loss of 5,000 Baluchi and 3,500 army lives.[36] In the present turbulence, the Pakistani army has, as before, played a major role, both in dealing with the protests of tribal leaders and, many Baluchis claim, in advancing its own interests at the expense of the province's inhabitants.

Baluchi political demands have tended to be somewhat incoherent, with different tribal leaders having different objectives. The clandestine Baluchistan Liberation Army demands the creation of an independent Greater Baluchistan, uniting Baluchi territories in Pakistan, Iran and Afghanistan. Other groups demand only greater provincial autonomy, with clearly delineated limits on the role of central government in the province. Still others advocate transforming Pakistan into a confederation in which each state would have the right to secede.

Islamabad maintains that Baluchi opposition is fomented primarily by three tribal families (out of around 77 high-ranking tribal families in total): the Bugtis and the Marris in the north, and the Mengals in the south. Musharraf's attitude towards all three was bullish: 'These elements should be wiped out of the country.'[37] In August 2006, eight months after the army resumed operations in Baluchistan after disturbances began again in 2005, the leader of the Bugti, Nawab Akbar Shahbaz Khan Bugti, was killed in an attack by the air force. Aged 79, he had been a governor and a chief minister of the province. Baluchis treated his death as a martyrdom, and the attack was widely viewed in the country as counterproductive and a step too far on the part of the authorities.[38] Four months later, Sardar Akhtar Jan Mengal, a leader of the Mengal tribe, was imprisoned. Actions such as these have been accompanied by reports of disappearances and forced population displacement in Baluchistan, though these have been difficult to verify because of restricted access to the areas concerned.[39] Most recently, in

April 2009, the president of the Baluch National Movement, Ghulam Mohammed Baloch, was found dead along with two other nationalist leaders soon after the three were detained by Pakistani security forces.[40] The discovery led to widespread anger and riots.

In January 2006, the chair of the Human Rights Commission of Pakistan reported the existence of 'a fully fledged military operation' directed at Baluchi protesters. Some 50,000 regular army and 30,000 paramilitary Frontier Corps personnel were reported to have been deployed.[41] Two months after the killing of Nawab Akbar Bugti later that year, US commentator and scholar of Asian affairs Selig S. Harrison described Pakistani army operations in the province as 'slow-motion genocide',[42] noting the use of F-16s and helicopter gunships to strafe villages, tactics that have also been used more recently in the FATA.

While Baluch tribal leaders have not been able to agree on ultimate political objectives, there is broad consensus on their grievances against Islamabad. Prominent among these are the way in which government revenues are distributed among Pakistan's provinces; the scarcity of employment in Baluchistan; and the violent and self-enriching behaviour of the army in the province.

Natural resources are a further source of tensions. Gas from Baluchistan accounts for 36% of Pakistan's total natural-gas production. The first gas deposits to be discovered in the province were found in the subdistrict of Sui in 1953, and geological surveys show that extensive reserves remain to be exploited. These have the potential to be a rich source of revenue, in the event that the province's political and economic climate became more favourable to investment, exploration and exploitation. Baluchistan also has large deposits of coal, silver, platinum, aluminium and uranium, as well as gold and copper mines operated by Chinese enterprises. In addition, the province could one day be on the route of gas pipelines running to India from Central Asia or Iran.

Its energy and mineral resources have, however, done nothing to increase the province's prosperity and stability, but have instead become a focus for grievances and allegations of dispossession. Only 17% of the gas produced in Baluchistan is consumed within the province, which receives just 12.4% of royalties. Only four of Baluchistan's 26 districts receive any gas at all. The provincial capital of Quetta was not connected by pipeline until 1986, and its eventual connection appears to have been linked to the establishment of a military garrison in the town. Gas produced in Sindh and Punjab fetches considerably higher prices, disproportionate to the costs of production.[43] Despite the benefits to central-government funds brought by Baluchistan's resources, and the relative poverty of the province's population, there has been little capital investment in health, education or other public services there. The severity of the province's water crisis, illustrated by the precipitous decline of 12 feet per year in the water table around Quetta at the turn of this century, has only been slightly mitigated in recent years by the discovery of a new groundwater source in the mountains behind the city. Meanwhile, little effort has been made to train or provide employment for Baluchis, with preference in the job market being given to 'imported' Sindhis and Punjabis.

Of the Baluchis' grievances, the baleful presence in the region of the Punjabi-dominated army alongside this neglect of the needs of the local population is perhaps the greatest source of resentment. Aside from the violence discussed above, the material gain the army has acquired in the province angers many Baluchis. The army's efforts to publicise the benefits to local people of development projects such as road-building are greeted with scepticism, as locals observe the construction of military cantonments – on land bought below the market price – to much higher standards than those available to them. In particular, the military presence in the districts of Kohlu and Dera Bugti (the site of natural-gas deposits) is seen locally as part of an ongoing expropriation of Baluchistan's natural resources.[44]

Gwadar

The wholesale and rapid development of the deep-water port of Gwadar on Baluchistan's southwest coast represents a substantial investment that promises to be of considerable benefit to Pakistan. In addition, the development provides a good illustration of the central government's behaviour in Baluchistan, and of local responses to it.

The project arose out of an exchange of visits between Musharraf and Chinese premier Zhu Rong Jhi in May and December 2001. Built mainly with Chinese capital and labour and costing around $2bn, Gwadar port has the potential to give China's navy a presence in the Indian Ocean, which could protect Beijing's oil-supply lines, as well as having other strategic uses. Due for completion in 2010, the renovated port will be able to receive tankers of almost 200,000 tonnes. A newly built township will include an industrial development zone. The port is to be linked by road and rail to Central Asia and Afghanistan, thus providing those countries with an outlet to the sea, as well as to Karachi by a 650km road.

Local Baluchis complain of a lack of consultation, the exclusion of provincial institutions and elected officials from decision-making about the project, land grabs by outsiders, and the exclusion of local labour and businesses from the employment and development opportunities offered by the project.[45] In February 2007, the federal government awarded a

40-year lease to the Maritime and Port Authority of Singapore to administer the port, with no prior consultation with provincial authorities.[46]

*   *   *

The problems in Baluchistan and the approaches taken to them by Islamabad echo those of other troubled regions of Pakistan. Fragile provincial and local institutions have remained under-developed in the province, and have been further weakened by minimal consultation from the centre and inadequate provision for the involvement of the local population in decision-making. The visible arm of the centre, in Baluchistan as in the FATA, has been the army, which is viewed as a Punjabi-dominated organisation that has little interest in the well-being of the province. Historically and currently, the army has proved ruthless in crushing dissent. Where financial benefit has come to Baluchistan, from, say, resource exploitation or revenue from the provision of transportation to NATO operations, it has been viewed as a by-product of the army's and the state's pursuit of their own material interests, and the share of profits that has remained in the province has been low.

With federal authorities tending to assume that locals cannot be relied upon to implement change themselves, and inadequate investment in education and training, among other factors, meaning that Baluchistan lacks skilled manpower, outsiders – Islamabad, the army, foreign interests – habitually make use of the province's economic and other resources with little regard for the potential and needs of its population, often using ruthless methods to achieve their aims. In the process, local opinion is further alienated, long-standing grievances are intensified, opposition increases and local development is thwarted.

As elsewhere in Pakistan, 'solutions' in Baluchistan will not be easy to come by. Taken together, the region's inaccessible and inhospitable terrain and the chronic material and educational deprivation of its tribal population, combined with its profound alienation from the centre, amount to formidable obstacles to progress in this strategically and economically important state.

The response of the centre has all too often made the task more difficult: the brutal response of the army to Baluchi challenges to central authority has aggravated resentments, as well as failing to eliminate violent opposition. Meanwhile, Islamabad's response to economic and social grievances has been largely limited to gestures. An aid package of Rs40.6bn ($580m) pledged to Baluchistan by President Zardari in 2009, for instance, was widely judged to be inadequate to the region's many needs. Of course, Pakistan's economic crisis sets limits on the money available, and external aid would be of much value in this regard.

But the root of much of the Baluchi feeling of unfair treatment lies in the system for distributing central funds to the provinces. Currently, the allocation of funds from the central budget to the provinces is calculated on a pro-rata basis according to population size, which makes no allowance for Baluchistan's poverty in comparison to, for example, the relatively prosperous Punjab. An overhaul of this inequitable arrangement might do much to ease the deprivation and resentment felt by Baluchis, and offset the perception that indigenous natural resources are being exploited to their disadvantage. Such a change would, however, need the consent of the Punjabi-dominated national assemblies, which for now at least seems a distant prospect. The issue is nevertheless one that Islamabad needs urgently to address. It is to be hoped that the increased attention being paid to Pakistan by outside powers concerned for its future might yet combine fruitfully with the increasing opportunities for public debate within Pakistan itself to stimulate such reform.

CHAPTER FOUR

Regional Relationships: India, China, Saudi Arabia and the Gulf

India

Since independence, India has been both Pakistan's arch rival, and the 'other' against which the country defines itself. Pakistan owes much of its identity to its distinctness from India. It has engaged in three sizeable wars with India, plus several major border clashes and skirmishes, and there have been numerous periods of high tension. The struggle over Kashmir has contributed to most of these conflicts. Pakistan, as we have seen, has sponsored decades of proxy paramilitary operations undertaken in the name of 'freedom fighting' designed to right or take revenge for cumulative wrongs. It has developed and deployed nuclear weapons whose sole strategic purpose relates to India. And it has used its relations with other countries, particularly Afghanistan and China, to promote its anti-Indian interests.

For its part, India has been far from passive. While the wars with Pakistan have been brief and in military terms decisive, with death tolls that were low by twentieth-century European standards, India's agencies too have engaged in violent covert operations, although with less visibility than Pakistan's and on a smaller scale. It was India that conducted the first nuclear test in 1974, which spurred Pakistan along a similar path, and India that first declared a nuclear-weapons capability after further tests in 1998, which Pakistan almost immediately replicated. India's methods for dealing with insurgencies in Kashmir, even allowing for Pakistani involvement in these, have often been brutal, inhumane and inconsistent with its claims to democracy.

Periodically, when particularly stung by Pakistani provocation, some Indian voices call for Pakistan to be decisively punished and broken up, with the remnants left to fend for themselves, so that this awkward country might finally cease to be an irritant to its vast neighbour. For some years after Partition there was also a view in India that Pakistan ought to be reincorporated into India, on the grounds that the 'two-nation theory', espoused by Jinnah, that Muslims and Hindus represented two thoroughly distinct political, as well as religious, cultures, and should therefore inhabit different states, was misguided. But such views have never prevailed. Just as Pakistan has an interest in promoting a cooperative regime in Afghanistan, India has not, ultimately, seen advantage in promoting anarchy and uncontrolled turbulence on its western border.

Kashmir

Much has already been written from many perspectives on the differences between India and Pakistan. Nevertheless, a brief summary is necessary here for an understanding of the events that have arisen from these differences and their current relevance. The issue of overwhelming importance has been Kashmir, the oldest dispute still before the United Nations.

At the time of India's independence, the ruler of the princely state of Jammu and Kashmir was presented with the three options open to all princely states, outlined earlier: to remain independent for a period, or to join either India or Pakistan.

But the position of this particular state was doubly delicate. Its large population and relative proximity to China and the Soviet Union gave it an unusual strategic significance. And while its ruler was a Hindu maharaja, more than three-quarters of its population was Muslim. In addition, the state was contiguous with both nascent countries, meaning that any of the three options might have been practicable, unlike, for example, in the cases of the former princely states of Hyderabad and Junagadh, which had Muslim rulers but which were deeper inside India, enabling India in effect simply to annexe them.

After Partition in August 1947, the maharaja, who was not popular with his subjects, temporised over the choices open to him. The precise train of subsequent events, including the role played by Lord Mountbatten, the outgoing British viceroy who went on to become governor general of independent India, is a matter of profound dispute between Pakistan and India. But some of the most important events are clear. In late summer and early autumn 1947, the violence surrounding the process of Partition spilled into Jammu and Kashmir and developed into a challenge to the maharaja's rule from many of his Muslim subjects. In October, several thousand armed tribesmen from NWFP entered the state. It is likely that these fighters had several motives for becoming involved: they may have wanted to fight in support of fellow Muslims against a Hindu ruler; either as part of this or separate from it, they may have wanted to force the maharaja into opting to join Pakistan; and, most simply, they may have had their eyes on the spoils of war. The maharaja sought help from India, signed an act of accession to India which was conditional on a subsequent UN-supervised referendum or plebiscite, and Indian troops entered the state to fight the incomers from Pakistan. A dispute about the order in which these last three events occurred lies at the heart of the competing claims.

Fighting continued throughout 1948 until the British, who still had officers commanding both armies,[1] brought about a ceasefire on 1 January 1949, by which point India controlled two-thirds of the state and Pakistan one-third. The ceasefire line was renamed the Line of Control by the Simla Agreement in 1972, soon after Pakistan's comprehensive defeat in its war with India in December 1971.

Pakistan claims that India moved in its troops before the maharaja signed the accession document, and that its actions were therefore illegal. Relying on the authority of resolutions passed by the UN Security Council, Pakistan for decades insisted on the need for a plebiscite to enable the people of the entire former princely state to decide which of the two countries to join (it recognised no third option of independence). The Pakistani position was that, until such a referendum was held, all the land covered by the former princely state was 'disputed territory'.

Over time, Pakistan has divided the parts of the former state that it now administers into the Federally Administered Northern Areas and Azad (Free) Kashmir, both of which are constitutionally distinct from the rest of the country. While Azad Kashmir has nominal autonomy, including its own constitution, the constitutional status of the Northern Areas remains undetermined. Both regions are indirectly ruled from the centre through the federal minister for Kashmir affairs and Northern Areas.

To add to the complexities, during a war between China and India in 1962, China annexed part of the former princely state, known as Aksai Chin, occupied by India. Pakistan announced a qualified recognition of the Chinese claim, and ceded additional territory in that region to China, which led to bitter complaints by India that Pakistan had given up territory to which it had no right and did not control.

India's formal position has been to claim rights over the entire former princely state of Jammu and Kashmir, including Azad Kashmir and the Northern Areas. While India recognises that there is a disagreement, it rejects the idea that the territory that it controls is 'disputed', and claims full sovereignty over it. What is now the Indian state of Jammu and Kashmir is divided for administrative purposes into three regions: Kashmir, which has a Muslim majority; Jammu, which has a Hindu majority; and the Ladakh region, geographically the largest of the three, where the majority of the sparse population is Buddhist and of a different ethnicity to the rest of the state's population.

Pakistan and India's official positions on Kashmir, each of which relates to the entire territory of the former princely state, have for many years appeared to outside observers to be incompatible with the reality on the ground as it has developed over the decades since the dispute began. There has seemed to be little prospect of progress so long as each country insists on a resolution in its favour.

A brief history of tensions

As well as Kashmir, there have been other sources of conflict and tension between India and Pakistan.[2] Several tense moments in the history of Indo-Pakistani relations have dropped out of the sight of many outside observers, but within the two countries, memories and narratives about them remain very much alive and, therefore, relevant to current Indo-Pakistani relations. It is not possible to treat here each of the numerous incidents and skirmishes at the Line of Control and other periods of heightened tension there have been over the decades, nor thoroughly detail the ongoing support by Pakistani agencies for the infiltration of militant insurgent groups into India, both across the line and by other routes.[3] But some of the more prominent peaks of tensions are outlined below.

In April 1965, there was a border clash between India and Pakistan in disputed marshland in the region of salt marshes and mud flats known as the Rann of Kutch on Pakistan's southeastern border. Later that year, Pakistan tried to induce an armed uprising in Kashmir, as a pre-emptive effort to counter a perceived rise in Indian power, as well as to advance its cause in Kashmir. India responded in September by sending regular forces over the international border. Pressure from the US and UK to halt the fighting and mediation by the Soviet Union persuaded each side to give up its territorial gains. The outcome of the conflict was, therefore, inconclusive militarily, though Pakistan's strategy was ultimately unsuccessful in that there was no change in the status of any part of Kashmir.

The 1971 war, in which the Indian Army intervened in East Pakistan during the civil war between Pakistan's west and east wings, was of a different order of magnitude. The immediate outcome was a thorough defeat for the Pakistani army in the east; Indian occupation of 5,000 square miles of Pakistani territory and capture of 94,000 Pakistani prisoners of war in the east; and a military standstill in the west. Following the subsequent secession of the east wing and the creation of the independent state of Bangladesh, India signed an agreement to withdraw from the territory it had occupied and release prisoners of war. In 1972, the two countries' leaders, Indira Gandhi and Zulfikar Ali Bhutto, met in the Indian city of Simla to make the agreement, which also resolved that differences between the two countries should be settled bilaterally and through peaceful means.[4] India has consistently maintained that this rules out third-party engagement in the Kashmir issue by means, for instance, of arbitration, mediation or facilitation.[5]

In 1984, the occupation by Indian forces of part of the Siachen Glacier in northeastern Kashmir highlighted a dispute about the route of part of the Line of Control which had remained without precise demarcation since the UN-supervised Karachi Agreement of 1949.[6] Several thousand troops from both countries have been deployed ever since in unforgiving terrain at altitudes of over 20,000 feet. But the military position remains a stalemate. More deaths have been caused by the fierce climate and conditions than by fighting. The territory has little or no strategic significance. Several ideas have been put forward for a peaceful resolution of the underlying issue, but any progress will be determined by the prevailing political climate.

In 1989, riots broke out between Hindus and Muslims in the Indian state of Jammu and Kashmir, with some Muslims demanding Kashmiri independence. The Indian authorities responded with violence. The Pakistani authorities encouraged and assisted the independence movement, which may have been partly influenced by the fall of the Berlin Wall and the first Palestinian intifada earlier that year, as well as by availability of mujahadeen who had been engaged in Afghanistan before the Soviet and US withdrawals in February. Around 140,000 Hindus fled violence in the Muslim-majority Kashmir Valley, some of whom joined refugee camps in Jammu. Tourism, the lifeblood of the region, declined in the years following the outbreak of violence, with visitor numbers falling from 80,000 in 1989 to 9,000 in 1995.[7] After about a year, however, it became clear that serious as it was, the insurgency was unlikely to escalate into significant bilateral military activity. Nevertheless, tensions continued for several years, and were exacerbated by the infiltration of militants from Pakistan across the Line of Control and repeated terrorist attacks in India more widely. Western interest in the region was sustained by the unusual incidences of kidnappings and murder of Western tourists in Indian-administered Kashmir in 1994 and 1995.

A period of gradual easing of tensions from 1996 was then interrupted by the mutual nuclear-weapons testing of 1998,

which began in the spring with five tests by India and its declaration of a nuclear-weapons capability, and continued with
Pakistan's rapid retort of six such tests, with which it matched
India's total, which included India's so-called 'peaceful' test of
1974.

Despite the tests, however, the easing of tensions resumed
for a time, with Prime Ministers Nawaz Sharif and Atal Behari
Vajpayee signing the Lahore Declaration in February 1999, to
widespread acclaim outside the region. The agreement envisaged, among other things, the resumption of bilateral dialogue
with a view to resolving all disputes, including Kashmir, by
peaceful means. But within months of the signature of the
agreement, the launch of Pakistan's military offensive over
the Indian side of the Line of Control near Kargil in Kashmir
soured relations once again. This misconceived and opportu-
nistic adventure initiated by Musharraf as chief of army staff
with the consent of Sharif was entirely at odds with the stated
objectives of the Lahore Declaration.

Tensions flared again in the aftermath of 11 September
2001. The October 2001 bombing of the Jammu and Kashmir
regional legislative assembly killed 38 people. In December
came the terrorist attack on the Indian parliament, in which
Pakistan-based militant groups Lashkar-e-Tayiba and Jaysh-e-
Mohammad were implicated. Both groups are believed to have
had support from the ISI in the past, though no evidence exists
of ISI involvement in this attack.[8] The ensuing mobilisation of
both countries' armies lasted for ten months.

India and Afghanistan
As we have seen, Pakistan has always viewed Afghanistan
through the prism of its antagonistic relationship with India,
attempting to use Afghanistan as its 'defence in depth' and
cultivating its mujahadeen as paramilitary reservists against

possible Indian threats. Above all, Pakistan has been concerned to ensure there is no threat from its western flank when its main concerns lie in the east. But Pakistan's concerns about Afghanistan in relation to India took on a new dimension when Musharraf decided to join the US-led Coalition in combating terrorism. When Musharraf concluded that it was necessary to aid the Coalition's efforts in Afghanistan and sever Pakistan's diplomatic ties with the Taliban, he was deeply apprehensive about the US policy of using the Northern Alliance to spearhead military operations in Afghanistan. For Pakistan, that policy involved an unholy mix of anti-Pakistan elements. The Pakistanis and the Northern Alliance, whose forces were led until his assassination in September 2001 by the Tajik Ahmed Shah Masood, regarded each other with intense suspicion. The Alliance had opposed the Taliban, whom Pakistan had until recently supported, and its leadership blamed al-Qaeda and the ISI for Masood's death.[9] From Pakistan's point of view, the Alliance was a group that had the support of old enemies, India and Russia, as well as its fickle friend the US. Pakistan's fear, therefore, was that its supporters in Afghanistan might be sidelined and that inimical interests would have free rein in the country.

Subsequent Indian activity in Afghanistan appeared to many Pakistanis to bear this fear out. India is Afghanistan's largest regional donor: since 2001, it has contributed $750m for reconstruction, pledging an additional $450m in August 2008. By mid 2008, there were around 4,000 Indian civilian and security personnel working in Afghanistan on relief and reconstruction projects, protected by the paramilitary Indo-Tibetan Border Police Force. India's assistance includes road-building, notably the Zaranj–Delaram highway in southwest Afghanistan near the Iranian border; helping to build Kabul's new parliament building; training Afghan police, diplomats and civil servants; and offering support in the health, education, transport, energy and telecommunications sectors. Pakistan has viewed this activity with dismay, its fear of encirclement compounded by India's establishment of a new airbase at Farkhor in Tajikistan.[10]

In a new development in 2009, India proposed that Pakistan agree to allow the transit of trucks from India to Afghanistan for humanitarian purposes. The aim appeared to be to deliver rice more quickly by avoiding the long sea and road route from Mumbai through Iran, possibly with a view to ensuring delivery in good time for the Afghan presidential elections due in August. For their part, the Pakistan authorities have complained about obstacles being put in the way of their own attempts to supply aid to Afghanistan.[11]

While India's help to Afghanistan might be viewed as a reasonable response to Afghanistan's clear needs, Pakistan sees it as a flagrant attempt to gain influence at its expense. It maintains that India's diplomatic presence in Afghanistan, in the form of an embassy in Kabul and consulates in Herat, Mazar-e-Sharif, Jalalabad and Kandahar, is well in excess of its legitimate needs, and that these sites are used as bases for directing anti-Pakistani covert activity in both Afghanistan and Baluchistan. In July 2008, the Indian embassy in Kabul suffered a car-bomb attack, thought to have been organised by the Haqqani insurgent network. The bombing, which killed at least 50 people, among them the embassy's defence attaché and its political counsellor,[12] was followed by allegations that official elements in Pakistan had a hand in the attack.

While both India and Pakistan have legitimate interests to protect in Afghanistan, the historic tensions between the two countries mean that, in Afghanistan as elsewhere, each country views the other's actions with intense suspicion and sees its hand in violent incidents and other disturbances. And indeed, the possibility of official collusion in incidents cannot be dismissed in all cases. If Afghanistan is not to join Kashmir as a stage on which Pakistani and Indian animosities are played out, both countries will need to recognise the other's sensitivities and make efforts not to inflame them.

Mumbai, November 2008

On the evening of 26 November 2008, ten terrorists began a series of coordinated attacks in Mumbai, India's largest city and its financial capital. Their ten separate targets included three hotels, Mumbai's massive railway terminus, a café with an international clientele, a Jewish community centre, a cinema and the port. Over the next 60 hours, the city was effectively paralysed. 164 people were killed and 308 wounded. Nine of the terrorists were killed.[13] Evidence from the one who was captured pointed to the involvement of Lashkar-e-Tayiba and its parent organisation Jamaat-ud-Dawa.

The Indian government quickly announced that the perpetrators had come from Pakistan, and that they had arrived by sea in hijacked boats. In early January 2009, when the Indian authorities dispatched a dossier of evidence to Pakistan, the Indian prime minister made a further claim, though he stopped short of specifying particular entities or individuals: 'There is enough evidence to show that, given the sophistication and military precision of the attack, it must have had the support of some official agencies in Pakistan.'[14] In contrast to its response to the attack on the Indian parliament in December 2001, however, the Indian government did not mobilise its armed forces. Instead, it put a freeze on the 'Composite Dialogue' that had been under way to resolve the differences between the two countries.

Pakistan was swift to reject the suggestion of official involvement, and emphasised its resolve to ensure that non-state actors did not use Pakistani soil as a base from which to launch terrorist attacks. The government's security adviser, Rehman Malik, announced that the authorities had closed down 87 institutions, including seven madrasas and eight relief camps belonging to Jamaat-ud-Dawa. A number of publications and websites were blocked and five suspected training camps closed, though Malik claimed that Pakistani authorities had not found any evidence of militant activity at the sites.[15]

Despite some apparently freelance denials by Pakistan's high commissioner in London, which were quickly disowned by the Pakistani prime minister, there can be little doubt that the perpetrators of the Mumbai attacks originated from Pakistan, and Islamabad has acknowledged that the single terrorist who survived was a Pakistani citizen. It would seem that Lashkar-e-Tayiba's violent advocacy of an Islamic caliphate poses a threat beyond Pakistan's borders as well as inside them. Although Pakistan had banned the group, along with other organisations, as far back as January 2002, there was little sign that the Pakistani authorities had invested much effort in trying to halt the activities of the organisations it had outlawed. This laxness may have been due in part to a wish to avoid a popular backlash from those who had benefited from the charitable activities of militant organisations, which often answered needs that the state proved unable to meet itself. Indeed, during the 2005 Kashmir earthquake, the various militant organisations entrenched in the region, among them Jamaat-ud-Dawa, proved more effective than any other organisation, the army included, in mobilising and delivering humanitarian relief.[16] This greatly enhanced such groups' popularity locally.

But another, darker, reason may also figure. There were rumours at the time of the earthquake that the ISI had facilitated the philanthropic activities of militant groups precisely in order to boost the groups' appeal and effectiveness with a view to bolstering their role as useful paramilitaries. As we

have seen, the army and the ISI have consistently been reluctant to alienate or eradicate militant groups, even when they
have run out of control, because of their utility in proxy operations against India. However, it is as yet uncertain as to whether
Indian allegations of continued Pakistani state involvement in
terrorist violence are based on current evidence or on extrap-
olations from past experience, as well as whether Pakistan's
denials were issued in good faith.

Distinct from such questions, suspicions have inevitably
arisen that the tension with India after Mumbai has in some
ways suited the army, as the possibility of a retaliatory attack
from India gives it a reason to move some of its troops away
from the troubling task of undertaking operations against its
own citizens in NWFP and the FATA, and possibly reduces
pressure from the US to do more in these difficult regions.

Before the Mumbai attacks, cooperation between India and
the US on counter-terrorism had not been close, despite the
transformation of their bilateral relationship in recent years.
Although both parties agreed that Pakistan was a major source
of terrorism and had somehow to be reformed, they could not
agree on the best strategies for achieving this. The US depended
on Islamabad to sustain the military operations against
al-Qaeda and in Afghanistan and therefore favoured a strategy
of unconditional engagement with Pakistan. In contrast, India
argued for an altogether tougher approach.[17]

The aftermath of the Mumbai attacks, however, saw unprec-
edentedly close cooperation between the US and India, with
collaborative efforts strengthening mutual ties. One well-
placed observer reported that the resources, technology and
professionalism of a team of specialists from the FBI and other
US agencies deployed to Mumbai to help with investigations
following the attacks evoked gratitude, admiration and even
envy in their Indian counterparts. The contribution of the US

analysts was deemed to have been essential to the assembly of evidence about the attackers and their methods, which has since been shared with other governments.[18]

Cooperation such as this suggests not only that the US shares India's concern to thoroughly investigate the roots of the Mumbai attacks but that, in helping India to resolve the issue by legal means, the US is keen to forestall a risky Indian response such as came after the attack on its parliament in December 2001. Any evidence of the involvement of Pakistani institutions that might emerge from these investigations could, by making the denial of uncomfortable connections between official organisations and militants much harder to maintain, be useful in attempts to prevail upon Islamabad to do more to eliminate terrorism originating from Pakistani soil.

Crisis management or conflict resolution?

With much outside encouragement, from the US and the UK in particular, Pakistan and India have over time deployed a range of traditional diplomatic instruments to try to manage their differences. A number of confidence-building measures were formulated during the tensions in Kashmir in the 1990s, some of which were put into practice, albeit in a piecemeal fashion. In 1997, following meetings between prime ministers, the two sides began the process known as the Composite Dialogue. This set up a formal procedure for the discussion of eight 'outstanding issues', of which Kashmir was one, within separate working groups. However, the process soon broke down over the question of whether Kashmir should be addressed as the 'core issue', as Pakistan advocated. It was revived again the following year and given new life by the Lahore Declaration and an accompanying memorandum of understanding in February 1999. But the Kargil conflict a few months later once again brought the dialogue to an abrupt halt. Because of his role in the Kargil operation, Musharraf was initially deeply distrusted, even loathed, by the Indian establishment when he assumed political power in October 1999.

It was not until the spring of 2003, after the period of crisis in 2002 following the terrorist attack on the Indian parliament, that tensions eased, diplomatic relations were restored, and more confidence-building measures were established. The Pakistani prime minister announced a ceasefire at the Line of Control in November 2003. In a breakthrough meeting with Indian Prime Minister Atal Behari Vajpayee in January 2004, Musharraf undertook to prevent the use of the territory under Pakistan's control (including Pakistan-administered Kashmir) 'to support terrorism in any manner'. The significance of this statement was heightened by the fact that it was the product of bilateral agreement through intensive back-channel diplomacy between two senior officials close to each country's leaders. The two leaders also agreed to resume the Composite Dialogue.

Gradually, both sides appeared to show signs of greater realism. Musharraf in particular seemed to recognise that India could not be dislodged from Kashmir through militancy and violence.[19] The general had a special interest in avoiding trouble in Kashmir at this juncture, preoccupied as he was with managing operations on the border with Afghanistan. In October 2004, having indicated ten months earlier that he was moving towards this position, he announced that Pakistan's traditional demand for a plebiscite on the region was impractical. He went on to call for a 'national debate' which might consider various options, including independence and joint control.

India initially reacted stiffly to such ideas, but soon appeared to become more accommodating. The country's new prime minister, Manmohan Singh, had had a productive meeting with Musharraf in September 2004, which he described as 'a new beginning'.[20] Singh later reiterated his willingness to look at all possible ways of resolving outstanding bilateral issues. At a further meeting the following April, the two leaders described the peace process as 'irreversible'.

Dialogue continued over the ensuing years, with many rounds of talks at an official level. The progress of parallel back-channel discussions led Pakistan's foreign minister, Khurshid Mahmood Kasuri, to claim in April 2007 that the two countries were extremely close to reaching a settlement of the Kashmir dispute. Media reports appeared to indicate that broad agreement had been reached on five elements: no change in the current division of Kashmir into Pakistani and Indian areas; the creation of a 'soft border' across the Line of Control (a loosely defined idea that appeared to envisage greater freedom of movement for people and goods); greater autonomy and self-governance for both the Indian- and Pakistani-controlled parts of Kashmir; the establishment of a consultative mechanism across the Line of Control; and demilitarisation of Kashmir at a pace determined by the rate of decline in cross-border terrorism.[21] The process of dialogue continued through 2007 and 2008, despite the political turbulence in Pakistan in 2007 that culminated in Musharraf's resignation, until it was stalled again by the Mumbai attacks in November 2008.[22]

Musharraf supporters and commentators and officials in India support the view that progress in the back-channel discussions had in 2008 reached a point where a modus vivendi was within reach, and conclude that if relations between India and Pakistan were to improve again the issue could, for all practical purposes, be resolved. This narrative that agreement over Kashmir was within reach also seemed to a great extent to be accepted by Western governments at the time.[23]

It is certainly true that, after their initial distrust of Musharraf, influential Indians came to believe that the general was a man with whom they could do business, and that Western governments were misguided in pressing for democratic elections that could lead to dangerous instability.[24] But the history of the Kashmir dispute suggests that there is a substantial gap between what might be agreed in principle between special envoys and what is actually deliverable in political terms. In addition, while Musharraf undoubtedly worked hard to persuade the US that he was making serious efforts to reduce the risk of conflict with India, and his 2004 renunciation of Pakistan's long-standing demand for a plebiscite in Kashmir did demonstrate a welcome flexibility, in practice, the efforts he was making towards a genuine accommodation may not have been as great as some US officials came to believe. In any event, the general's deep unpopularity in the later years of his leadership and the growing strength of militant groups would have encouraged domestic opposition to making any significant changes to Pakistan's long-standing position on Kashmir. Crucially, it was also far from clear that Musharraf would have secured the backing of the committee of his corps commanders, whose support would have been essential.

Within India, it was similarly unclear whether Singh would have been able to sell the kind of agreement then under consideration to his disparate and fragile coalition, let alone to an opposition dominated by a Hindu nationalist party. Even had he done so, Indian commentators and politicians would have been strongly tempted to present the agreement as a victory for India. India could not be seen to be making concessions to a military autocrat: any deal would need to be portrayed at the very least as a Pakistani recognition that the issue had to be managed quietly for an indefinite period with no change of sovereignty or, most provocatively, as a Pakistani capitulation. Any such response on the part of India would most likely have scuppered any agreement, since no Pakistani government could allow itself to appear to have accepted a humiliating political defeat from India. In view of all this, a senior Pakistani source closely engaged in the back-channel negotiations expressed doubts in late 2007 about the likelihood of an agreement.[25]

Kashmir and beyond: what is the political reality?
The debate over sovereignty in Kashmir centres on the Kashmir Valley in the Indian-administered part of the region, which is the home of the Kashmiri language and was once a popular destination for tourists attracted by the valley's natural beauty and handicrafts. None of the other regions of the former princely state has the same popular association with 'Kashmiriat', or the 'essence' of Kashmir. Some 95% of the 3.5 million inhabitants of the Kashmir region of Jammu and Kashmir (of which the Kashmir Valley is the main geographical component) are Muslim.

As time passes, any expectation that India might actively seek to gain possession of 'Azad Kashmir' or the Northern Areas appears less and less realistic. For all their special constitutional arrangements, these areas have become dependent on Pakistan, which has subsidised them for decades. Nor could Pakistan realistically aspire to administer the Jammu or Ladakh regions, not least because some 65% of Jammu's 4.5m people are Hindus and most in sparsely populated Ladakh are Buddhists.[26]

But even if it were politically feasible to distil the substance of the dispute down to the Kashmir Valley, the issue would probably remain intractable. India feels no obligation to make any concessions on an issue as resonant as sovereignty to a neighbour that has pursued its cause through violence and other dubious methods. In addition, the views of the valley's population, who would need to be consulted in the event of any change in status, are by no means clear-cut: a proportion, who claim to owe no allegiance to either Pakistan or India, argue for independence, which is widely regarded as impracticable and unsustainable. As well as the people currently living in the valley, there are also those who have left or been forced out of the region. The composition of the valley has changed radically since the UN Security Council resolutions of the 1940s that first called for a plebiscite. There must now be considerable room for dispute over who now constitute 'the people of Kashmir', and whose views should be taken into account.

All efforts so far to resolve or manage the differences between Pakistan and India over Kashmir and other issues have been contaminated by suspicion: that words have not matched deeds; that India has regarded process as an acceptable substitute for progress; that Pakistan has engaged in double-dealing; that commitments will not be deliverable. Whenever there has been a setback, discussion has been dogged by recrimination and the reiteration of painful history. Paradoxically, and despite the 60-year history of violent disagreement, senior representatives of both countries persist in maintaining that, living in such close proximity with one another with, in some cases, close family ties across the border, each side understands the other very well. To many outsiders, there appears to be plenty of evidence that this assumption represents a spectacular misjudgement which has too often led to dangerous misunderstandings.

Crucially, there remain grounds for serious doubt about whether a policy advocated by an elected government in Pakistan could be implemented if the leadership of the country's army opposed it. Self-styled 'guardian of the nation', the Pakistani military has an acute feeling of vulnerability in relation to India. India's army is triple the size of Pakistan's, its air force five times as large and its navy six times as large. All are within easy reach of Pakistan's major cities, including Karachi and Lahore. Opinion in the upper echelons of Pakistan's army is exceptionally difficult for outsiders to assess. But it remains of decisive importance to the question of how to manage the difficult relationship between the two countries.

Musharraf's replacement as chief of the army staff, General Kayani, is clearly more considered in his public language than his volatile predecessor. And he has taken welcome steps to distance the army from national politics. Nevertheless, it cannot come as a surprise that India is unwilling to accept Pakistani denials of any involvement by official Pakistani organisations in the Mumbai attacks. Even if there was no such involvement, there are legitimate questions to be addressed about what exactly Pakistan will now do to ensure that the consequences of its earlier actions are fully and finally brought under control.

Perhaps the best that can be hoped for in the medium term is that Pakistan and India's differences can be managed in such a way that they cease to present a risk of conflict between the two nuclear-armed powers. The hitherto ill-defined notion of a 'soft border' in Kashmir would seem to be the most promising avenue to be explored here, along with the continuation and development of measures designed to reduce tensions and dispose of as many minor irritants as possible. There seems little scope for direct third-party involvement in settling the Kashmir dispute so long as India continues to reject this outright. But other states can continue to play a role in easing tensions between the two countries, as they did when the two armies were mobilised in 2001–02. And more needs to be done to prevent Indo-Pakistani rivalries in Afghanistan from infecting relations further.

China

Faced with a serious economic crisis, it was perhaps natural that President Zardari's first official state visit after his inauguration should be to Beijing. However, as we have seen, Pakistan's long-standing friend and ally was to disappoint, unwilling to help Pakistan keep its pledge not to report to the IMF. China's relationship with Pakistan, while still close, is shifting.

After some initial suspicion owing to Pakistan's alliance with the US in the early 1950s, China moved closer to Pakistan as its relations with India deteriorated, with war breaking out between China and India in 1962. By the end of 1963, when Pakistan ceded territory around Aksai Chin to China, Pakistan and China had settled their border disputes, and China was soon to prove to be a reliable source of diplomatic, economic and military support. The relationship blossomed for all to see with the completion in 1978 of the strategically important Karakoram Highway, which connects Pakistan's Northern Areas to China's Xinjiang Province via the Kunjerab Pass, a feat of engineering that Musharraf has called 'the eighth wonder of the world'.[27] It was down this road, flanked by vertiginous drops and prone to blockages by landslides, that China supplied hundreds of mules for use by the mujahadeen against the Soviet occupation of Afghanistan in the 1980s.[28]

For China, its relationship with Pakistan has served as a hedge against India. Given that China and India have their own disputes over hundreds of miles of border and other issues, it has been convenient for China that the Kashmir dispute has tied up so much of India's security forces and attention.[29] It was during the 1962 conflict with India that China first officially declared its support for Islamabad's advocacy of a plebiscite in Kashmir. Pakistan also provides China with a bridge to the Muslim world, a conduit into South Asian strategic space and, most recently, maritime access to the Gulf through the port at Gwadar.

The most politically significant aspects of China's cooperation with Pakistan have been in the military and nuclear fields. In the 1970s China supplied arms, including tanks, naval vessels and combat aircraft, in a $600m programme, and constructed a tank-repair and production factory at Taxila near Islamabad and an air force repair facility at nearby Kamra.[30] In January 2008, the Taxila facility became the site of the serial production of the jointly developed JF-17 *Thunder* aircraft, the programme for which Musharraf announced on Independence Day, 14 August 2006.[31] The first batch of aircraft was delivered in 2007; 150 more are reported to have been ordered and an eventual total of 250 is possible.

In 1976, two years after India conducted its first nuclear test, Zulfikar Ali Bhutto entered into an agreement with China on nuclear cooperation which he described as 'my greatest achievement and contribution to the survival of our people and our nation'.[32] Many Pakistani nuclear scientists received training in China. In 1983, China transferred to Pakistan a complete nuclear weapon design and began helping to operate Pakistan's uranium-enrichment plant at Kahuta.[33] Assistance included the supply of ring magnets for Kahuta and equipment for a nuclear reactor under construction at Khushab.[34] In 1986, the two countries concluded a comprehensive nuclear cooperation agreement; China began helping Pakistani scientists to enrich uranium to weapons grade and transferred enough tritium for up to ten warheads. As Sino-Pakistani nuclear cooperation developed, it caused increasing concern to the US, which imposed successive sanctions on China over the course of the 1990s in connection with alleged contravention of the Missile Technology Control Regime and the supply of goods relating to weapons of mass destruction.

China also helped Pakistan to develop weapon-delivery systems. Pakistan's HATF missile systems, first tested in 1988, were built with Chinese help, as were its longer-range *Shaheen* systems tested in 1999, which were developed from Chinese missiles.[35] (The *Ghauri* system is probably based on the North Korean *No-dong-1*.)

Trade between the two countries, which amounted to around $3 billion in 2007, has more than trebled since 2001, though it remains well below its potential and is massively in China's favour. It is supplemented by large-scale barter trade and smuggling from China.[36] A free-trade agreement, which came into force in July 2007, aims to increase bilateral trade further. When Musharraf visited Beijing in April 2008, he and his hosts reaffirmed the target of a five-year cooperation plan to increase Sino-Pakistan trade to $15bn. China has also been a significant source of direct investment. In 2007, it was Pakistan's third-largest foreign direct investor, investing around $700m, or 17% of Pakistan's total foreign direct investment, a little more than the US's contribution and more than double that of the UAE.[37] The development of Gwadar port advances China's political, commercial and potentially strategic interests within this context of increasing economic engagement. As with the Karakoram Highway, Chinese labour is being used in the construction of Gwadar, thereby significantly reducing China's foreign-exchange and other costs.

But, as was brought home to Zardari in October 2008, Chinese cooperation with Pakistan has not been without limits. During Pakistan's civil war and conflict with India in 1971, China spoke of its commitment to Pakistan's unity, but never showed any sign of intervening militarily in support of it. More recently, as China has gradually entered the international mainstream, its attitude towards nuclear cooperation has begun to shift. By 1996, China had formally pledged not to supply equipment to unsafeguarded facilities. Although civilian nuclear cooperation has continued, China was dismayed by the revelations that followed the break-up of A.Q. Khan's illicit nuclear-supply network, and appears to want to portray itself as a responsible international stakeholder in this context.

Though China has tended to support the Pakistani position on Kashmir, when Pakistani troops violated the Line of Control during the Kargil expedition in 1999, Beijing was unequivocal that the line should be respected. This position was no doubt influenced by an awareness of the dangers of a confrontation between two nuclear powers. But it may also have reflected a shift in Sino-Indian relations, as China's role as a rising world power means that it increasingly has wider interests to attend to, which transcend its relationship with Pakistan.

China is also concerned about the spread of Islamist militancy in and around Pakistan, and the risk that China could become infected by it. Muslim Uighur separatists in Xinjiang province are among those fighting in Afghanistan and can be found in some extremist enclaves in Pakistan's tribal regions. China made fierce representations to the Pakistani government in July 2007 when Chinese sex workers were held hostage by extremists in Islamabad's Red Mosque, and again in August 2008, when Chinese technicians were abducted and murdered in Pakistani territory.

Instead of providing unconditional funding of the magnitude of the $5bn sum that Zardari may have been seeking, the joint statement signed during the president's Beijing visit in October 2008 was replete with diplomatic niceties and 'framework agreements', and less than specific about any concrete help.[38] It was only after Pakistan had reached its agreement with the IMF that China made a $500m loan to Pakistan to help rebuild its foreign-exchange reserves.[39]

But despite the adjustments to China's strategic assessment of Pakistan, the bilateral relationship remains valuable to both sides. As China has an interest in reducing militancy, there may be scope for the US to persuade China of the benefits of more proactive engagement to influence Pakistan. China might be more open to such persuasion if the US were able to assure it that it had no aspiration to establish long-term military bases in the region, and that a substantial reduction in the threat of terrorism from the region would facilitate early US military withdrawal.

Saudi Arabia and the Gulf

If the precise outlines of Pakistan's relationship with China are not always fully clear, the country's relations with its Arab co-religionists are even more opaque. Pakistan and the countries of the Gulf have many interests in common, rooted in a shared cultural and religious heritage and multiple personal and economic networks, as well as strategic and military connections. The complex and intertwining relationships that exist reach well beyond what is documented in official statistics. It is clear that large sums of money have entered Pakistan from both official and unofficial sources in Saudi Arabia in particular, as can be seen in the many mosques in the country built with Saudi help. But little is known about the quantities of funding or the precise purposes to which it is put, and neither country provides details of any bilateral military connections.

Pakistan, Saudi Arabia and the Gulf states are all members of the Organisation of the Islamic Conference. And while all try to keep their ties with Iran as normal as possible, Pakistan and the Arab countries also share concerns about the possibility of Iran encouraging unrest among their Shia minorities and about Iran's nuclear ambitions. At a social and economic level, some three million Pakistanis live in the Gulf and Saudi Arabia, remitting around $3bn to Pakistan in the financial year 2006–07. Total trade between Pakistan and Gulf Cooperation Council countries stood at $11bn in 2006.[40]

While it is difficult to judge the precise reach and influence of the political and religious connections between Pakistan and its most valued Arab partner, Saudi Arabia, these are clearly substantial.[41] Saudi Arabia has supported Pakistan politically in its wars with India and over the Kashmir issue. It strongly endorsed Zia-ul-Haq's Islamisation programme. During the Soviet occupation of Afghanistan, it provided more than half the funding for the jihad, joining the funding from the US and others that was channelled through Pakistan. The Saudis developed close links with the ISI as soon as the Soviets invaded Afghanistan in 1979, paying the organisation large subsidies and, with the support of Prince Turki, the head of the Saudi General Intelligence Department, helping it to resist civilian oversight. Then, in 1995–96, as the Taliban emerged, Saudi religious police tutored and supported the group as it built up its own Islamic police.[42] Strains developed in 1990, when some Pakistani politicians and then-Chief of Army Staff General Mirza Aslam Beg spoke out in support of Saddam Hussein and the invasion of Kuwait. But fences were mended with time and Pakistani effort. The UAE, Saudi Arabia and Pakistan were the only states to recognise the Taliban rule in Afghanistan up until its collapse in 2001.

Saudi Arabia has over the years provided Pakistan with loans, gifts and subsidised oil, and it contributed $600m to the relief effort following the 2005 earthquake in Kashmir. Although details are elusive, expert observers believe that official aid is matched by large investments from Saudi princes and religious institutions. Saudi funds have sponsored many of Pakistan's madrasas, as well as Islamabad's Faisal Mosque and religious groups in Afghanistan and Pakistan.

Rumours about Saudi connections with Pakistan's nuclear programme have a long history. It has been suggested that Zulfikar Ali Bhutto sought financial help for the programme from Saudi Arabia in the early 1970s and that King Faisal obliged in return for a promise that Pakistan would provide a nuclear umbrella for the kingdom.[43] In 1977, Bhutto changed the name of the city of Lyallpur (named after a British colonial administrator) to Faisalabad in the king's honour.

The nuclear connection emerged more clearly in 1998, when the US imposed sanctions on Pakistan and India in response to their nuclear-weapon tests. Though Pakistan's smaller and less self-reliant economy suffered more, it seems that the effects of the sanctions were to some extent offset by a Saudi decision to set up a special account for Pakistan to provide it with oil at a reduced price. Shortly after Pakistan's tests that year, Saudi Defence Minister Prince Sultan visited Pakistan and toured its nuclear and nuclear-missile facilities. A.Q. Khan visited Saudi Arabia in November 1999. It was around this time that US officials expressed concern that Pakistan might furnish Saudi Arabia with a nuclear weapon. After Crown Prince Abdullah visited Pakistan in October 2003, there was speculation – rebutted by both countries – that there had been a secret agreement that, in return for cheap or free oil, Pakistan would provide Saudi Arabia with nuclear technology to enable it to have a deterrent against Iran.[44]

Pakistan has provided conventional military aid and expertise to Saudi Arabia, beginning in the 1960s with help to the Royal Saudi Air Force to build and fly jet fighters. In 1969, Pakistani Air Force pilots flew Royal Saudi Air Force *Lightnings* that repulsed a South Yemeni incursion across the kingdom's southern border.[45] In the 1970s and 1980s, up to 15,000 Pakistani troops were stationed in Saudi Arabia, some in a brigade combat force near the Israeli–Jordanian–Saudi border. In 2006, Pakistan offered to sell 150 main battle tanks to the kingdom, which might have allowed Saudi Arabia to reduce its dependence on the West for much of its weaponry, though so far this proposal does not appear to have progressed. Close ties between the two countries' militaries continue today.

Saudi Arabia has also been heavily engaged in recent Pakistani politics. The Saudis have long-established ties with the Sharif family, who shared their support for Zia's Islamisation policy. With US help, they persuaded Musharraf that Nawaz Sharif should go into exile in the kingdom for ten years after the coup in 1999. When the US and UK persuaded Musharraf to allow Benazir Bhutto to return in October 2007, the Saudis judged that it would be impossible to keep Sharif in the kingdom against his will. They summoned Musharraf, and Sharif was allowed to return to Pakistan.

When Zardari unsuccessfully petitioned Riyadh to allow Pakistan to defer payments for oil in November 2008 following the disappointing visit to Beijing the previous month, it is possible that part of the reason for Riyadh's reluctance to help lay in the close relationship of the al-Sauds with Sharif, Zardari's political rival.

Clearly, the Saudi government takes a close interest in Pakistan, an interest it pursues through its financial resources and political influence. Some Saudi help, such as the favourable pricing of oil, has been of evident benefit to Pakistan. Other kinds of assistance, for example the official and private Saudi funding of radical madrasas, have had a malign effect. The precise extent of Saudi Arabia's influence on Pakistani government policies and behaviour is unclear, as is the extent to which Pakistan's leaders have sanctioned, or even been aware of, the full scope of Saudi activities in the country.

*   *   *

All Pakistan's neighbours – India, Afghanistan, Iran, China and, across the Arabian Sea, Saudi Arabia and the Gulf states – have substantial interests in Pakistan. Some of these interests, such as the sectarian preoccupations of Saudi Arabia and Iran and the strategic interests of India and China, may be mutually conflicting, and their pursuit could have destabilising effects on Pakistan. But these countries also share a fundamental interest in the maintenance of Pakistan as a stable state. This shared interest offers the possibility that, for all their differences, Pakistan's neighbours might to some extent be willing to join other interested countries in helping Pakistan emerge from the exceptional turbulence of recent years.

Prospects and Policies

In recent years Pakistan has suffered from an infection of violent disorder and insurgency, mainly pursued in the name of a politicised brand of religion which many Muslims, including the great majority of Pakistanis, do not recognise as their own. But Pakistan is not a lost cause, 'close to a tipping point', nor is its army, as some have feared, at risk of being 'overwhelmed by terrorism'.[1] There is no prospect that extremist religious parties will gain control of the country as a whole, through the ballot box, by force of arms or by terror. Nonetheless, the threats to other countries that emanate from Pakistan are real and may worsen. Pakistan's challenges run deep. Attempts at any quick fixes to these will prove fruitless, costly and counter-productive.

The ultimate objective

Pakistan's vision for itself was set out in 1949, in a parliamentary 'objectives resolution' which was enshrined in the country's constitution in 1985.[2] This vision has generally been expressed as amounting to 'enlightened moderation'[3] and a modern, democratic Islamic state, the achievement of which has proved elusive. Western governments have articulated their own objectives for the country. President Obama's declared aims for Pakistan and Afghanistan are limited and specific: to disrupt, dismantle and defeat al-Qaeda and the Taliban.[4] They do not say much about Pakistan more broadly. The British aim is wider: the emergence of a stable, economically and socially developed democracy. But though unexceptionable, this provides little guidance to practitioners.[5] And there is a clear potential tension between the two objectives of stability and democracy, as the US and UK implicitly recognised in their overlong support for Musharraf. Beyond the mere articulation of such a goal, the real question is about the manner in which such an ideal scenario might be brought closer.

There are three broad possible approaches to achieving lasting stability as an alternative to the current turbulence. These may be described as containment, stabilisation and transformation. Ultimately, nothing less than transformation will enable Pakistan to achieve the objectives to which successive military and civilian governments in the country have purported to aspire, and prevent it from remaining a source of threats to itself and to other countries. Containment and stabilisation will need to be steps along the way, but are not in themselves sufficient. Such a target is ambitious, would be costly, and some of the necessary changes may take a generation or more to achieve. Furthermore, this kind of change cannot be imposed from outside, as Western states' attempts in 2003–04 to implement their own vision for Iraq have shown. The main driving forces would need to be the people and institutions of Pakistan. But considerable external help would be necessary, with engagement by countries both within and outside the region.

At least until 2009, when Obama announced his new combined strategy for Afghanistan and Pakistan, the United States' approach towards Pakistan appeared to be focused mainly on containment, dealing with specific threats and challenges as they arose or as opportunities to tackle them presented themselves. The main instruments were military – the provision of training and equipment, and the selective use of force. Public and private exhortations, first to Musharraf and then to Zardari's administration, to do more to try to destroy al-Qaeda and combat Afghan and, latterly, Pakistani insurgency and terrorism, accompanied large-scale military-related assistance.[6]

These methods clearly failed to meet US objectives and contributed to dangerous reactionary movements in Pakistan. Senior Pakistani ministers and officials, during Musharraf's tenure and subsequently, angrily and accurately remarked that Pakistani security forces had suffered more casualties than had all NATO forces in Afghanistan, and that Pakistanis believed that the country was 'fighting Washington's war'.

The military-focused approach included the wooing of the army with sales of equipment irrelevant to the Afghanistan campaign, and was accompanied by blatant but ultimately futile attempts at political manipulation. Designed to promote compliance with US objectives, the approach was also no doubt intended to produce short-term stability. Since Pakistan's civilian political class was so flawed, the Bush administration appeared to judge that its interests in Afghanistan would be best served by acquiescing in a dominant role for the army, despite its condemnation of military rule when Musharraf took over in 1999. But the support shown by the US, and to a lesser extent the UK, for Musharraf's autocratic regime continued well beyond the stage where the general had lost legitimacy at home. The rationale of ensuring short-term stability also lay behind the fateful deal between Musharraf and Benazir Bhutto brokered by the US and the UK in 2007, which was widely viewed in Pakistan as cynical interference. And, after Bhutto's assassination, the notion of containment lay behind the US's patent preference throughout 2008 for Zardari, despite his widespread unpopularity, over Nawaz Sharif, whom US officials initially cold-shouldered.

Some gross tactical errors of judgement on the part of the US further alienated Pakistani opinion and made matters worse. The unexpected arrival in Islamabad of Deputy Secretary of State John Negroponte in March 2008, for instance, just as newly elected Prime Minister Gilani was forming his government, and the ground assault by US special forces in South Waziristan in September of that year both appeared to be motivated by short-term tactical objectives: in the first case, to exert influence on the newly elected government, and in the second, to neutralise certain military targets. But the resulting outrage among politicians and wider Pakistani opinion had damaging strategic consequences. Such overt interference and violation of Pakistan's sovereignty insulted Pakistani national honour and, in the second case, stimulated *badal*, the Pashtun obligation to avenge blood. Resentment was fuelled, violent opposition to US involvements was strengthened and mobilised, and it became harder for Pakistan's politicians – whatever their actual intentions – to be seen to respond positively to the US.

The clearest problem with this expedient approach was the contradiction between shoring up compliant authoritarian leaderships on the one hand and the declared support for democracy on the other. So long as the army's power was sustained, even a responsible elected administration would struggle to develop a shared sense of nationhood and move the country towards long-term stability.

The elements of the 'comprehensive new strategy for Afghanistan and Pakistan' launched by President Obama in March 2009 that relate to Pakistan represent an advance on the practice of the Bush administration. By pressing both the US

Congress and other countries to give more aid to Pakistan's civil sectors, and by emphasising that his objectives could not be achieved 'with bullets or bombs alone', Obama distanced himself from the previous overemphasis on military-related assistance.[7] But elements of the new approach predate the current administration, such as the proposal for more civilian aid to Pakistan, which had, in the form of the Kerry–Lugar Bill, been approved by the Foreign Relations Committee in July 2008, and had been before Congress for some time before that. And the president's stated goal of eliminating al-Qaeda is too limited. A combined approach to the problems of Afghanistan and Pakistan does not amount to a strategy towards Pakistan. The threats emanating from Pakistan go well beyond al-Qaeda, and a strategy that focuses on that group will surely fail to adequately tackle these wider threats.

It is essential to acknowledge that Pakistan's links with terrorism, its possession of nuclear weapons and the fragility of its state are issues of fundamental importance, both in the region and well beyond. And it must be recognised that these issues require special and sustained attention. The objective can be nothing less than a transformation of a situation that had by 2009 generated simultaneous political, security and economic crises. Pakistan needs to revisit the pluralistic and democratic goals of its founding father, Jinnah, and work to establish a durable and unthreatening sense of identity; break free from its 30 years of politicised religion and distorted politics; and recalibrate the role of the army and intelligence services in relation to the body politic and civil society. Beyond containment and stabilisation, the vicious cycle of non-democratic elected governments alternating with military rule needs to be broken. Elected politicians need to fulfil their constitutional responsibilities, and should not be impeded by interference and manipulation from the army and intelligence services.

Pakistan must offer real social and economic opportunities for its population, and present alternatives to extremist militancy.

An objective of transformation cannot and should not be imposed by outsiders. It must be brought about by Pakistan itself: its government, electorate, administrators and civil society. But the resources and political influence of other countries will be essential. External assistance, if offered in an appropriate way, should not be dismissed as interference or neocolonialism. Though it is difficult to measure such things with any precision, a multitude of sources of information about opinion within Pakistan, among them the country's media commentary, its political discourse and opinion polls,[8] the strong public reaction that was seen in mid 2009 against the activities of the Pakistani Taliban in Swat and the outcome of the February 2008 general election (which represented a clear rejection of both Musharraf's 'King's Party' and the alliance of religious parties), all suggest that a majority of the population – perhaps a very great majority – feel their country's current condition to be intolerable and wish to see it transformed.

While this is a formidable challenge, and Pakistan is much more populous than Afghanistan, the transformation of Pakistan is more feasible than the transformation of Afghanistan. For all its diversity and internal tensions, apart from in the FATA, Pakistan has long traditions of central and provincial governance and of trading and entrepreneurship; its infrastructure, agriculture and natural resources are reasonably well developed. All of these assets have been eroded over the past two or three decades, to a great extent by poor management. But each could be strengthened, in some cases quite quickly, if the security and political environment were more permissive. Increased and well-directed external investment, especially in major energy and water projects, could bring rapid and visible benefit. This in turn could help to reduce instability and create space for the necessary political reforms.

The US is likely to remain the most powerful, although not the only, external source of influence and material assistance. But its influence within Pakistan will be severely limited so long as Pakistanis judge, based on past experience, that Washington will turn its back on Pakistan once it has achieved its primary objectives. Refuting the accusation that the US is never more than a fair-weather friend will require high levels of non-military support to be sustained in spite of inevitable political vicissitudes. Reducing military-related demands on Pakistan by, for example, rerouting the convoy routes that currently run from Pakistan's southwest coast through Peshawar to Afghanistan would do much to reduce the US footprint in Pakistan, and the resentment it provokes.[9] Once it becomes clear that friendship with the US brings real benefit and opportunities, Pakistan should become more receptive to US advice and influence.

For their part, the institutions and people of Pakistan need to exercise the necessary determination if they are to transform their situation. For too long, much of Pakistan's political discourse has appeared to take refuge in the notion that the country's difficulties are the fault of others, brought upon it by actions of which Pakistanis do not approve on behalf of interests they do not share. This attitude may have been part of the reason why the parliament formed in early 2008 failed to craft a strategy or policies for dealing with the range of insurgencies that by that time were posing direct challenges to the Pakistani state. Instead, despite their disapproval of military rule and the army's over-involvement in politics, civilian politicians relied excessively on the army and its judgements for policy decisions. This reliance on the military lay behind Islamabad's consent to expedient dealing-making with insurgents for short-term apparent security gains.

However, the dramatic consequences of one such accommodation, the February 2009 agreement between Pakistani government officials and the outlawed TNSM, whereby official sharia courts would be established in the Malakand division in exchange for peace in the region, radically changed public and political sentiment. The TNSM's disregard for its obligation to deliver peace in exchange for the sharia concession and its brutal interpretation of sharia law appalled both locals and the wider Pakistani public. As a result, the military operations in Swat and Waziristan in mid 2009 were underpinned, for the first time, by widespread support from both the general public and the political class. If such support for counter-insurgency can be sustained, and if Pakistan's leaders can develop a coherent political strategy that incorporates it, there will be real grounds for hoping that a wider transformation might, with time and effort, become attainable.

A false alternative

Rather than taking a long-term cooperative approach, some commentators have suggested that, if Pakistan continues to fail to put its house in order, the US should employ greater coercion and fundamentally alter its relationship with Islamabad.[10] During the US presidential campaign, Obama appeared to show some sympathy with this approach when he, along with other candidates, suggested that the US should increase its unilateral military action against terrorists in Pakistan, in a statement that provoked a great deal of publicity and controversy.[11] Analysts who advocate a new, more forceful strategy point to the fact that the US has provided Pakistan with billions of dollars in support since 2001 (described by some as 'US generosity'[12]), but has received little benefit in return. If, they argue, such inducements continue not to achieve the desired result, a more challenging approach should be pursued, in tandem with more unilateral action on the part of the US. This approach might involve, for example, tying US aid and US support for IMF and World Bank programmes for Pakistan to progress on defeating Afghan insurgents and their support networks (thus explicitly linking attempts to improve the lives of Pakistanis with the goal of meeting US military objectives). Such tactics would be accompanied by greater pressure on Pakistan's leaders to crack down harder on violent insurgency in Baluchistan, NWFP and the FATA.[13]

The idea of taking a more coercive approach to Pakistan has two serious weaknesses. Firstly, it fails to take account of the fact that the injection of large amounts of costly military assistance, which the donor may regard as 'generosity', is seen by the recipient as self-interested manipulation that brings with it more cost than benefit. The US will lack moral authority in Pakistan, and will certainly receive little gratitude, so long as it is seen as acting exclusively in its own interest and appears to attach only secondary importance to the interests of Pakistanis. This is especially the case as the US has signally failed to demonstrate how its military and military-related activity in Pakistan and Afghanistan has brought any improvement in the condition of the Pakistani people. Secondly, the approach risks alienating a country that Washington has described as an ally. If the US were to become more coercive in its dealings with Pakistan, this could induce Pakistan to begin to distance itself from the US, a process that might, if attempts at coercion were kept up, lead to direct animosity between the two countries, with unforeseeable but surely highly dangerous consequences.

The current US approach, in line with Obama's new policy, amounts to a mixture of increased use of force through more frequent drone attacks in the FATA, and the promise of more aid to the civil sector, in accordance with the proposals of the Kerry–Lugar Bill on non-military support to Pakistan. It is less coercive than supporters of a more forceful approach might advocate – Obama does not, for instance, propose the use of ground forces in the FATA or in Quetta, the base of Afghan leadership council the Quetta Shura. But the announcement of a policy that includes aid to the civilian sector is not sufficient: the real test is to turn that policy into practice. If the US were to fail in this, and were either to continue to appear to focus on its military objectives at the expense of the needs of Pakistanis, or to turn its back on Pakistan as it has in the past, either through exasperation or because certain military objectives in Afghanistan had been met, the threats to Western interests within Pakistan could well grow.

It was only in 2009 that outsiders began belatedly to recognise the severity of the threats that emanate from Pakistan, as events in the country became too dramatic to be ignored. This recognition must now compel the US and others to shun both these risky options and work together with Pakistan over the long term to effect a transformation in the country's situation.

Operational objectives

The shortcomings and limitations of past policies are clear. The key question is how the transformation of Pakistan advocated here might be brought about. It is of course impossible to be confident about the prospects for success, which will be determined by the complex intersection of the actions of those within and outside the country, and the willingness of all concerned to exercise a degree of political will that has hitherto been lacking. But the alternatives are so bleak that there can be no option but to make the attempt.

More optimistically, the turbulent events of the past five years may yet give rise to a determination on the part of Pakistan's politicians and Pakistani society more broadly to tackle the serious shortcomings in the country's governance. While the weak performance of the government that was elected to such optimism in February 2008 and the obstructive behaviour of the main opposition party might give little cause to expect any rapid change in the country's political habits, it is not unreasonable to hope that the combination of a public increasingly impatient with the country's deteriorating political and security situation and the provision of constructive external help might encourage positive policy changes.

The army's decades-long influence in politics and civilian affairs needs to be addressed as a high priority. Currently, with the rise in violence in the country, the military is heavily occupied with the conduct of operations and undergoing associated donor-sponsored mentoring and training schemes, and is probably thus less liable than it has been to involve itself in the political process. There is also some cause for optimism about reform: public discontent over the army's role in politics following nine years of military rule, and the evident wish of the army under General Kayani to reduce its political profile as a result, offers a rare opportunity for an elected government to begin rebalancing the distribution of power. Such change must be undertaken sensitively and gradually, not least because the army must continue to fulfil essential duties: rapid and radical change would be destabilising. But change there must be. There can be little doubt that the political parties would like to bring this about. But to do so effectively will require careful consideration and, for all the difficulties and risk of obstruction this entails, close consultation with the army itself.

In particular, attention should be paid to the task of injecting life into either the Defence Committee of the Cabinet or the National Security Council,[14] two essentially duplicate bodies set up as consultative and decision-making forums to ensure ongoing government oversight of the military. While such mechanisms have been weak in the past, some kind of bridging group to ensure that lines of communication between civilian government and the military remain open will be crucial and, with the necessary will on the part of governments, existing mechanisms could be strengthened sufficiently to play a vital role in moderating army influence.

As regards external support for reform in general, since it is all of Pakistan that needs to be assisted – not least so that a sense of national unity and shared identity might eventually emerge – no province must be neglected. An exclusive concentration on the tribal regions would risk increasing resentment and instability throughout the country by reinforcing the perception that donors are occupied only with Afghan- and military-related issues.

Nonetheless, the deprivation and propensity for violence of the tribal regions mean that account must be taken of the special nature and needs of these areas. It is unrealistic to contemplate any early development of industry in the FATA, or exploitation of any potential mineral resources. But job-creation schemes might be established in neighbouring NWFP and Baluchistan which could attract workers from the FATA as well as locals, thus generating income and new opportunities for FATA residents, as well as for people in NWFP and Baluchistan. A modification of the system for distributing budgetary funding to the provinces towards a more needs-based system would also do much to assuage both Pashtun and Baluchi resentment. It would be necessary too to improve the administrative systems relating to the FATA, primarily by rebalancing the power in the region away from the military and back towards civilian control through the political agents. This could be achieved in part by recruiting high-quality personnel to the role of agent, as in the decade or so following Pakistan's independence. The question of the future constitutional status of the tribal areas, though important, is too sensitive for external prescription.[15]

It should be left to Pakistan to decide on both the manner and timing of any change. But this need not prevent external legal and constitutional experts from offering objective advice on the legal aspects of bringing about change in practice.

Throughout the country, aid workers and diplomats offering assistance need to operate as close to the ground as possible. Their skills should include knowledge of local languages and an awareness of local history, custom and social norms. This will help them to avoid advocating policies and processes that conflict with local culture. For its part, Pakistan's government would do well to make maximum use of the country's increasingly vibrant civil society, including the media and judiciously selected non-governmental organisations, both in the process of generating support for reform and for advice on and help in implementing new programmes. The Pakistani diaspora, too, can be engaged as a source of skills and funding. Donor countries should give high priority to training and mentoring indigenous administrators, at federal, provincial and district levels. Any resulting reinforcement of Pakistan's institutions and democratic instruments will help to reduce the country's dependence on the army.

The security sector, including the judiciary, the police and the intelligence services, needs special attention and reform. Its evident shortcomings understandably discourage the tribal regions from altering their existing arrangements, despite the flaws of the Frontier Crimes Regulation, and relinquishing sharia law in favour of the federal system. The highly visible protests by lawyers in 2007–09 against political manipulation of the legal system offer hope that support for reform might come from within this sector. External financial assistance and intellectual exchange could further boost the reformist role of the legal community. The police could benefit from the considerable body of international expertise in police reform that has been developed in other places over the past two decades. Improvements in remuneration, training and conditions of service could also prove highly beneficial and reduce the temptations of corruption and extortion.[16] Greater governmental control of the intelligence services will inevitably be difficult to achieve, and they should not be emasculated. But such change will be essential if the ISI is to help control terrorism rather than support it. While it seems likely that Musharraf's attempts from 2001 to submit the ISI to more control from the chief of army staff had the effect of bringing the organisation under closer supervision, concerted effort will be required to ensure the prime ministerial oversight that nominally exists becomes a reality.

Strengthening the instruments of democracy, including through updating electoral rolls and working to develop the autonomy, integrity and competencies of the Electoral Commission, could help to build voter confidence and thereby increase participation in elections. Over time, the cumulative effects of electoral reform, greater electoral participation and an increasingly active media and civil society could in turn bring positive changes to Pakistan's political culture. With such changes, Pakistani governments might – and certainly should – become more alive to the importance of re-examining and regularising the country's constitution, which has suffered from the many dubious amendments made to it by Musharraf and his predecessors, and might too acknowledge the need to reform some of the country's most regressive statutes, notably the Hudood Ordinance. Independent expert advice on constitutional matters has been requested and given in Pakistan in the past, and its increased provision could help a willing government to make such changes.

Pakistan's primary education and health care systems have been neglected and underfunded by successive governments.

More external funding and attention to chronic managerial weaknesses could help to build capacity here. In education, improved schooling would offer poor families an alternative to madrasas, some of which incubate violent extremism. Real progress on public health and education would enhance the standing and authority of the state.

Tackling water scarcity, which is partly a result of inadequate storage and wasteful distribution systems, and correcting inequities in water distribution, would reduce resentments and the attendant risk of violence. Economic growth between 2001 and 2007 highlighted the severity of Pakistan's energy shortages, and losses of power, which led to street protests in 2008 and 2009, remain a source of popular frustration. Greater investment in power generation and, especially, the exploitation of existing gas, coal and mineral resources would bring employment and other economic benefits. In each of these areas, external funding and expertise could reinforce central government action. Pakistan's agricultural, textile and garment sectors offer substantial opportunities for job creation and foreign-exchange revenue. Western governments should urgently consider the possible advantages of offering preferential access to their markets.

The state's ability to respond to the challenge of dealing with the 3.4 million people estimated to have been displaced by the army's offensives in Swat and North Waziristan in mid 2009, and to mobilise funding from external donors to help in this task, will have crucial implications for popular confidence in state institutions and thus for stability nationally. In this context it is important to keep in mind the extent to which the prestige of militant groups such as Jamaat-ud-Dawa was boosted at the expense of that of the civil administration as a result of their relief efforts after the 2005 Kashmir earthquake.

Western governments need to develop closer professional relations with the Pakistani armed forces. Training schemes and regimental exchanges should be resumed. The isolation imposed by the US after 1990 produced a 'lost generation' of officers who had no experience of training or cooperation with the armed forces of other countries and who therefore had no opportunity to learn about the relationships between military and civil institutions elsewhere. It will be equally essential, however, that Pakistan's elected civilian leadership ensures that development of the army's capabilities does not further enhance its influence over civilian institutions, and that its excessive share of the national budget is progressively reduced in favour of the social sector.

If this array of policies is to bear fruit, donors and Pakistan's institutions will need to develop coherent and coordinated strategies in order for the necessary high levels of external funding to be disbursed effectively and transparently. The appointment by several interested countries in early 2009 of special envoys to Pakistan and Afghanistan offers a possible mechanism for greater coordination – provided that envoys do not compete with one another or succumb to the temptation to over-promote their national interests at the expense of Pakistan's sustainable stability. Further streamlining to avoid the complications of dealing with a multiplicity of donors is also desirable. The task of coordinating the selection of priorities and administering external support might be taken on by one of the international financial institutions, which are accustomed to working with Pakistan and are well placed to recruit administrators and field workers.

While being careful to remain pragmatic and focused on 'the art of the possible', donors must also go beyond traditional bilateral development-cooperation models in their relationships with Pakistan to take fuller account of the multiple connections between development needs, security, politics and governance. Military security, diplomacy and development cannot be kept separate.

A more coordinated approach would also increase donors' leverage over Pakistan. To ensure accountability, donors must insist on a high degree of transparency about the use of their funding. The absence of such transparency during Musharraf's regime created much ill will and jeopardised further US military aid. Funding and other assistance should be calibrated as much as possible according to the effectiveness of its application, with good progress reinforced and doubtful practices disfavoured. Donors' efforts will be appreciated increasingly as their assistance begins to show results. Positive progress on development and reform programmes should itself gradually increase Pakistan's absorptive capacity and improve administrative practice. Similarly, as donors' engagement increases and outsiders gain knowledge and understanding, their efforts can take better account of Pakistan's institutional strengths and weaknesses. However, precisely because of these institutional weaknesses, initial progress will be slow, and there are likely to be serious setbacks along the way. Projects may also fail as a result of opposition from vested interests, bad practices and general human frailty, as well as for technical reasons or because of administrative inadequacy. Patience and perseverance will be essential on all sides.

Possible obstacles

Three issues in particular – Kashmir, the Durand Line and the question of negotiating with 'the Taliban' – have attracted much discussion, and merit attention here. Some commentators have suggested that resolution of the first two issues would be the key to most of Pakistan's problems, and that they should therefore be high priorities for external attention.

The reality, however, is not that 'solutions' relating to Kashmir and the Durand Line are prerequisites for the cure of Pakistan's ills, but that attitudes and practices in Pakistan, including the dominance of the army, will need to be transformed before any resolution of these issues will be possible (and, of course, attitudes in India and Afghanistan too will need to change).

On Kashmir, in spite of the optimism among many contemporary observers about the prospect of a modus vivendi being reached, it was never clear that the kind of agreement that was under consideration in the back-channel negotiations between India and Pakistan of 2003–07 would have received the support it needed from either the Pakistani army or India's ruling coalition. Even if the necessary support had emerged, it is likely that a triumphalist celebration of any agreement that cast it as a Pakistani capitulation would prove irresistible in India, and would have the effect of making Islamabad withdraw its support. The Kashmir issue, like so many international sovereignty disputes, is not susceptible to rapid resolution, but needs instead to be carefully managed so as to minimise the likelihood of it erupting again as it has done so frequently before.

Regarding the Durand Line, there is a view, favoured by some NATO military commanders, that an early resolution of the status of the line would do much to settle the tribal regions and put an end to decades of bitter squabbles between successive Afghan and Pakistani governments. The establishment of an agreed and recognised international border, so the argument goes, would help to control movement in both directions, and would thwart ISI efforts to maintain a 'Talibanised belt' in the FATA.[17]

Such a formalisation of the line's status would certainly be welcome to many in Pakistan. While Pakistan rejects outright the notion that the Line of Control that divides Kashmir in the east of the country should be recognised as a permanent international border (the back-channel negotiations on Kashmir did not come close to reaching an agreement on the issue of the line), officially at least, it takes the opposite view of the line that divides the Pashtuns in the west. Those in Pakistan who are eager to solidify the existing boundary firmly dismiss Afghan leaders' rejection of the line's legal validity. It has even been suggested that the US Special Envoy Richard Holbrooke might become a latter-day Durand and provide for a fence along the length of the line.[18] But the Durand Line, like Kashmir, is an extremely sensitive issue, and any attempt to resolve it in a precipitate manner would meet such opposition among the 30m Pashtuns in the region that pursuit of the more immediate objectives of building better governance and improving security in the region would be severely impeded.

There is currently no apparent will within the Pakistani government to address the disputed nature of the line in a more careful and conciliatory manner, nor to embark upon negotiations with Afghanistan on the issue. Indeed, a threat made by Musharraf in 2007 to erect a border fence along the line was repeated by Gilani in July 2009.[19] External pressure to find a negotiated resolution of the matter would thus find little favour. Hopes for a lessening of tensions over the Durand Line must, therefore, not be pinned on achieving a resolution that is not currently in prospect, but focus instead on efforts to generate employment and improve governance in the tribal regions so as to gradually reduce local communities' sense of grievance and render the dispute less salient over the long term.

Opposition to 'negotiating with the Taliban', an article of faith among many politicians and analysts outside Pakistan, is too rigid a position to apply to the complex reality of the tribal regions.[20] The term 'Taliban' is often used loosely, and covers a wide variety of actors, including some who have no wish to negotiate and others who may have very little in common with the groups usually associated with the Taliban name. Most of the major agreements reached in Waziristan and Swat in the past few years have conspicuously failed. But this may tell us more about the circumstances in which the agreements were reached than about the principle of seeking accommodation. Whether it would ever be desirable or indeed feasible to attempt to negotiate with an Afghan Taliban leader such as Mullah Omar would depend on whether he was ready to change his outlook and do business with an elected Afghan or Pakistani government. At present that seems highly unlikely. And, since Pakistani 'neo-Taliban' leaders such as Baitullah Mehsud and Maulana Fazlullah appear determined to oppose the state by force, then force may be the only means with which to neutralise them. Judicial instruments should be used to deal with those who are motivated by criminal interests. But there are also many currently opposing the Pakistani state and Western interests in Pakistan who seek primarily to avenge harm done to them or their tribe, or have other grievances. Representatives of the state should be prepared to engage in discussion with such people in the company of tribal elders, using the traditional methods of resolving disputes and agreeing compensation for wrongs that have hitherto received scant consideration from those outside the tribes themselves. Despite the erosion of the influence of such methods, if handled with care and sensitivity to tribal sensibilities, these could yet prove effective in resolving many of the grievances that exist, thereby narrowing the range of dispute.

International support

While US financial resources will be essential to the realisation of Pakistan's transformation, US influence will be no less necessary in engaging other countries. India, China, Saudi Arabia, the Gulf countries and Iran could all potentially play important roles. The US will need to work to mobilise and coordinate the common interest of Pakistan's neighbours in subduing violent instability in their region. While Arab funding for Pakistani madrasas has frequently brought great social benefits, more effort is needed to halt funding that leads to subversion or violent militancy. The increasingly nuanced approach taken by China over the past decade or so towards Pakistan, seen in its disapproving response to the Kargil episode and recent expressions of concern about hostage-taking and violence towards Chinese citizens in Pakistan, might be harnessed to reinforce the concerns of others. The US could encourage New Delhi to project greater understanding for Pakistani concerns about real or imagined Indian activities in Afghanistan and Baluchistan, as well as encouraging both India and Pakistan to manage their differences, including those over Kashmir, with restraint. And, despite the fraught US–Iran bilateral relationship, the US also shares interests with Iran, in the areas of reducing anti-Shia sectarian violence and narcotics smuggling.

However, the world should not expect the US to shoulder all the financial and administrative burden of assisting Pakistan. In addition to its unwelcome contribution to Pakistan's nuclear-weapons programme, China has furnished two highly visible monuments to its history of cooperation with Pakistan: the Karakoram Highway and the soon-to-be completed port of Gwadar. Gulf Arab countries also make considerable contributions, although since the donors generally prefer not to reveal the purposes to which these funds are put, these seldom appear in Pakistan's budget. Remittances from the Pakistani diaspora are also of great value to Pakistan's economy. But even taking account of these examples, foreign support has not been commensurate with the challenges that are potentially posed to foreign interests if Pakistan is left in its unstable current state.

Some EU countries have sizeable aid programmes in Pakistan. The UK, a notable example, contributes to Pakistan partly for historical reasons and because of its large British Pakistani community. But the performance of the EU as a whole has been lamentably weak.[21] The pledges made at the Pakistan Donors' Conference in Tokyo in April 2009 and the convening of the first EU–Pakistan Summit in June 2009 suggest that the EU recognises the need for improvement, but it will need to rise to the challenge of transforming its promises into reality.[22]

* * *

Pakistan has become gravely weakened over the last decade. This is to a great extent a consequence of chronic domestic problems that date from the country's earliest years: the failings of the political class, the army's dominance and pursuit of its own interests, and the vicious cycles of authoritarian rule. But Pakistan has also paid a heavy price for other countries' behaviour towards it, notably the West's accommodation with the country's military rulers in the 1980s and its encouragement of a jihad in the service of Cold War strategic goals. The resulting abiding mistrust of the US and other countries is epitomised by one Pakistani retort to those outsiders who declare that Pakistan's nuclear weapons are unsafe: 'I say that you're making them unsafe. When you were not in the region, there was no problem.'[23]

Much of the power of this widely held view lies in its kernel of truth: the coincidence of the five-year rise in insurgency in Pakistan and the ongoing US-led military campaigns in Afghanistan and now within Pakistan itself makes it difficult to argue that outsiders' military operations have no negative impact on Pakistan's internal security. But the role of outsiders is, of course, only part of the story. As regards nuclear dangers, the relationship between Pakistan's development of nuclear weaponry and its rivalry with India, the country's history of proliferation and its failings of governance have been central to concerns about Pakistan's nuclear security. More broadly, the country's manifold domestic shortcomings illustrate the breadth of the challenges that Pakistan's own leaders are responsible for tackling.

There are now signs, among them the recent public reaction against the actions of Pakistani Taliban in the tribal regions, that opinion in Pakistan is increasingly impatient with growing instability and has begun to move towards the view that the country needs urgently to put its own house in order. Indeed, only Pakistani institutions can ultimately accomplish the necessary changes. But they will not be able to do so without external counsel, financial help and the input of a broad range of concerned outsiders. The situation demands prolonged, intensive and well-directed effort on the part of both Pakistan's institutions and its people, and the many other countries that have an interest in what happens to this troubled country.

GLOSSARY

ANP	Awami National Party
FATA	Federally Administered Tribal Areas
IJI	Islamic Democratic Alliance
IMF	International Monetary Fund
ISI	Inter-Services Intelligence (Directorate)
JI	Jamaat-e-Islami
MMA	Muttahida Majlis-e-Amal
MQM	Muttahida Qaumi Movement
NAB	National Accountability Bureau
NWFP	North West Frontier Province
NADRA	National Database and Registration Authority
NRB	National Reconstruction Board
PATA	Provincially Administered Tribal Areas
PML	Pakistan Muslim League
PML(N)	PML(Nawaz)
PML(Q)	PML(Qaid-e-Azam)
PPP	Pakistan People's Party
SSG	Special Services Group
TNSM	Tehrik-e-Nifaz-e-Shariat-e-Mohammadi
TTP	Tehrik-e-Taliban Pakistan
UAV	unmanned aerial vehicle

NOTES

Introduction

1 Jeremy Page, 'Google Earth Reveals Secret History of US Base in Pakistan', *The Times*, 19 February 2009.

2 Richard A. Oppel, 'Strikes in Pakistan Underline Obama's Options', *New York Times*, 23 January 2009.

3 For fatality figures, see for example 'US and Coalition Casualties: Afghanistan', CNN.com, http://edition.cnn.com/SPECIALS/2004/oef.casualties/, which cites 1,238 International Security Assistance Force deaths by July 2008. A Pakistani army source puts Pakistani army losses up to October 2008 at 1,400: 'Exclusive Dispatch: Pakistan's Hidden War', *Independent*, 23 October 2008, http://www.independent.co.uk/news/world/asia/pakistans-hidden-war-969784.html.

Chapter One

1 H.V. Hodson, *The Great Divide* (London: Hutchinson & Co, 1969), p. 580.

2 After Indonesia and just ahead of India. There is some dispute about the order, with some suggesting that India's Muslim population is larger than that of Pakistan.

3 Ian Talbot, *Pakistan: A Modern History* (London: C. Hurst & Co, 1998), p. 13.

4 S.P. Cohen, *The Idea of Pakistan* (Washington DC: Brookings Institution, 2004), pp. 205 and 207.

5 Owen Bennett-Jones, *Pakistan: Eye of the Storm* (New Haven, CT: Yale University Press, 2002), p. 270.

6 Talbot, *Pakistan: A Modern History*, pp. 275–6.

7 Steve Coll, *Ghost Wars* (London: Penguin Books, 2005), p. 44.

8 Talbot, *Pakistan: A Modern History*, pp. 248 and 267.

9 For a graphic and emotional account of the US relationship with Pakistan, see Tariq Ali, *The Duel* (London: Simon & Schuster, 2008). See also Dennis

Kux, *The US and Pakistan, 1947–2000* (Baltimore, MD: Johns Hopkins University Press, 2001).

[10] See for example Mirza Aslam Beg, 'Emerging Union of Pak-Iran and Afghanistan', *Pakistan Observer*, 4 January 2009, http://pakobserver.net/200901/04/Articles03.asp. In the same article, Beg also suggests that 'the callous bloodbath of Mumbai on 26 November was enacted by RAW [the Research and Analysis Wing, India's external intelligence agency], CIA and Mossad, – the Saffron Nexus – to defame Pakistan in the comity of nations and lend justification for punitive action'.

[11] Mohammad Yousaf and Mark Adkin, *The Bear Trap: Afghanistan's Untold Story* (London: Leo Cooper, 1992), p. 81.

[12] Talbot, *Pakistan: A Modern History*, p. 267.

[13] Pervez Hoodbhoy, 'Politics of Islam', occasional paper presented to a private IISS meeting, 20 April 2007.

[14] Coll, *Ghost Wars*, p. 175.

[15] Talbot, *Pakistan: A Modern History*, p. 268.

[16] Cohen, *The Idea of Pakistan*, p. 108.

[17] Coll, *Ghost Wars*, p. 175.

[18] *Ibid.*, p. 180.

[19] The ceasefire line between the Indian- and Pakistani-administered parts of Kashmir following the 1947–49 war came to be called the Line of Control under the terms of the 1972 Simla Agreement.

[20] Ahmed Rashid, *Taliban: Militant Islam, Oil and Fundamentalism in Central Asia* (London: IB Tauris, 2000), p. 21.

[21] Coll, *Ghost Wars*, p. 283.

[22] Rashid, *Taliban: Militant Islam, Oil and Fundamentalism in Central Asia*, p. 29; Coll, *Ghost Wars*, p. 291.

[23] Rashid, *Taliban: Militant Islam, Oil and Fundamentalism in Central Asia*, p. 23.

[24] 'Afghanistan: Funding of NGOs', House of Lords *Hansard*, 25 February 1999, cols 1233–5, http://www.parliament.the-stationery-office.com/pa/ld199899/ldhansrd/vo990225/text/90225-01.htm.

[25] Duncan Gardham, 'MI5 Chief Warns of Threat from Global Recession', *Daily Telegraph*, 7 January 2009, http://www.telegraph.co.uk/news/newstopics/politics/defence/4144460/MI5-chief-warns-of-threat-from-global-recession.html.

[26] Conversation with Pakistani officials, 2001.

[27] Pervez Musharraf, *In the Line of Fire* (New York: Free Press, 2006), pp. 209–11.

[28] Coll, *Ghost Wars*, p. 480.

[29] Musharraf, *In the Line of Fire*, p. 88.

[30] Talbot, *Pakistan: A Modern History*, p. 411.

[31] *Ibid.*, p. 295; Mateen Haider, 'ISI Closes its Political Wing', Dawn.com, 23 November 2008, http://www.dawn.com/2008/11/23/top3.htm; Cohen, *The Idea of Pakistan*, p. 178.

[32] Lawrence Ziring, *Pakistan at the Crosscurrent of History* (Lahore: Vanguard Books, 2004), p. 210.

[33] Talbot, *Pakistan: A Modern History*, p. 287; other non-Pakistani historians and analysts have written in similar terms.

[34] *Ibid.*, pp. 293 and 309.

[35] Ziring, *Pakistan in the Twentieth Century* (Oxford: Oxford University Press, 1999), p. 524.

[36] Talbot, *Pakistan: A Modern History*, p. 311.

[37] Bennett-Jones, *Pakistan: Eye of the Storm*, p. 233.

[38] Ziring, *Pakistan in the Twentieth Century*, p. 527; Talbot, *Pakistan: A Modern History*, p. 312.

39   Ziring, *Pakistan in the Twentieth Century*, p. 535.

40   Talbot, *Pakistan: A Modern History*, p. 317.

41   *Ibid.*, p. 321.

42   *Ibid.*, p. 329; Ziring, *Pakistan in the Twentieth Century*, p. 541.

43   Talbot, *Pakistan: A Modern History*, p. 326.

44   Ziring, *Pakistan in the Twentieth Century*, p. 548.

45   *Ibid.*, p. 565.

46   Ziring, *Pakistan in the Twentieth Century*, p. 571; and Bennett-Jones, *Pakistan: Eye of the Storm*, p. 235.

47   Ziring, *Pakistan in the Twentieth Century*, p. 572.

48   Bennett-Jones, *Pakistan: Eye of the Storm*, p. 36.

49   Cohen, *The Idea of Pakistan*, p. 150, Bennett-Jones, *Pakistan: Eye of the Storm*, p. 238.

50   M. Ziauddin, 'Bill Has to Cover Two More Stages', *Dawn*, 10 October 1998, http://www.pakistani.org/pakistan/constitution/amendments/15thamendment_stages.html.

51   Bennett-Jones, *Pakistan: Eye of the Storm*, p. 18.

52   The tension between Sharif and Musharraf and the lead-up to Musharraf's coup are vividly described in *ibid.*, pp. 37–48.

53   Bennett-Jones, *Pakistan: Eye of the Storm*, p. 237, quoting Iqbal Akhund, Bhutto's foreign-affairs adviser.

54   *Ibid.*, pp. 230–31.

55   Robin Cook, October 1999.

56   Mudassir Raja, 'IHC Sets Aside Convictions in Gilani Corruption Cases', 5 February 2009, http://www.dawn.com/2009/02/05/top5.htm.

57   See Nathan Associates, 'Pakistan: Economic Performance Assessment', produced for review by USAID, September 2007, p. 24, http://www.nathaninc.com/nathan2/files/CASProjects/DOWNLOADFILENAME/000000000036/Pakistan 2007 Economic Performance Assessment.pdf.

58   Shaun Gregory, 'The ISI and the War on Terrorism', *Studies in Conflict and Terrorism*, vol. 30, no. 12, December 2007, pp. 1,013–31.

59   Shuja Nawaz, *Crossed Swords* (Oxford: Oxford University Press, 2008), p. 373.

60   Yousaf and Adkin, *The Bear Trap: Afghanistan's Untold Story*, pp. 1 and 22.

61   Gregory, 'The ISI and the War on Terrorism'.

62   Nawaz, *Crossed Swords*, pp. 411–13.

63   Sean P. Witchell, 'Pakistan's ISI: The Invisible Government', *International Journal of Intelligence and Counter-Intelligence*, vol. 16, no. 1, Spring 2003, pp. 380–1; Gregory, 'The ISI and the War on Terrorism'.

64   Nawaz, *Crossed Swords*, pp. 452, 467–9, 472–3, 482.

65   *Ibid.*, pp. 479, 534.

Chapter Two

1 Musharraf, *In The Line of Fire*, p. 201.

2 UN Security Council Resolution 1373, 2001.

3 For 2002 to 2007, the US concluded foreign military-sales agreements with Pakistan worth $4.55bn. The equipment to be paid for from Pakistan's hard-pressed budget included a number of '"big-ticket" platforms more suited to conventional warfare' than to counter-terrorism operations. Apart from 18 F-16s, an aircraft with a long and controversial history in the region, which can be used in counter-insurgency operations, these included 500 AMRAAM and 500 *Sidewinder* air-to-air missiles, 100 *Harpoon* anti-ship missiles and six close-in naval guns, as well as other equipment and armaments, the costs of which have been shared between the US and Pakistan. See 'Major US Arms Sales and Grants to Pakistan Since 2001', prepared for the Congressional Research Service by K. Alan Kronstadt, specialist in South Asian affairs, 3 June 2009, http://www.fas.org/sgp/crs/row/pakarms.pdf.

4 Nathaniel Fick, *One Bullet Away* (London: Weidenfeld and Nicolson, 2005), pp. 101–10.

5 This phrase emerged again during a visit to NWFP in 2002, in a conversation with a former senior member of the ISI who had observed a number of such interactions.

6 'Afghanistan: National Opinion Poll for BBC, ABC News and ARD', BBC press release, 9 February 2009, http://www.bbc.co.uk/pressoffice/pressreleases/stories/2009/02_february/09/afghanistan.shtml.

7 Talbot, *Pakistan: A Modern History*, p. 395.

8 P.R. Chari, Pervaiz Iqbal Cheema and Stephen P. Cohen, *Four Crises and a Peace Process* (Washington DC: Brookings Institution Press, 2007), p. 273. This provides an authoritative and detailed account of events that were little known outside governments at the time.

9 *Ibid.*, p. 163.

10 The speech is summarised in 'Musharraf Speech Highlights', BBC News, 12 January 2002, http://news.bbc.co.uk/1/hi/world/south_asia/1757251.stm.

11 Musharraf, *In the Line of Fire*, pp. 87–98.

12 Reuters report, 31 May 2002, quoted in Zahid Hussain, *Frontline Pakistan*, (London: IB Tauris, 2007), p. 109.

13 Mark Mazzetti, 'Behind Analyst's Cool Demeanor, Deep Anxiety Over American Policy', *New York Times*, 26 December 2008, http://www.nytimes.com/2008/12/27/washington/27riedel.html?_r=1&scp=1&sq=riedel&st=cse.

14 Talbot, *Pakistan: A Modern History*, p. 399.

15 See 'Declaration of the Presidency on Behalf of the European Union on the General Elections in Pakistan', 15 October 2002, http://europa.eu/rapid/pressReleasesAction.do?reference=PESC/02/155&format=HTML&aged=0&language=EN&guiLanguage=en; 'EU Finds Flaws in Pakistani Vote', VOA News.com, 12 October 2002, http://www.voanews.com/english/archive/2002-10/a-2002-10-12-14-EU.cfm?moddate=2002-10-12.

16 Ahmed Rashid, 'Jihadi Suicide Bombers: The New Wave', *New York Review of Books*, vol. 55, no. 10, 10 June 2008, http://www.nybooks.com/

articles/21473; Hasan Askari Rizvi, 'A Difficult New Year', *Daily Times*, 4 January 2008.

17 Parliamentary and presidential elections are not directly related to one another. Constitutionally, the president is elected by the two national and four provincial assemblies, while parliament is chosen by the electorate.

18 Private conversations, New Delhi, December 2007 and subsequently.

19 Carlotta Gall, 'Musharraf Wins Vote, But Court Will Have Final Say', *New York Times*, 6 October 2007, http://www.nytimes.com/2007/10/06/world/asia/06cnd-pakistan.html?_r=1&hp.

20 Shamim-ur-Rahman, 'Benazir Calls it Martial Law on Dash Back Home', *Dawn*, 4 November 2007, http://www.dawn.com/2007/11/04/top6.htm.

21 Carlotta Gall and Salman Masood, 'Ex-premier of Pakistan Arrested on his Return', *New York Times*, 10 September 2007, http://www.nytimes.com/2007/09/10/world/asia/10cnd-pakistan.html?_r=1.

22 Talbot, *Pakistan: A Modern History*, p. 400.

23 Jane Perlez and Salman Masood, 'Bhutto's Widower, Viewed as Ally by US, Wins the Pakistani Presidency Handily', *New York Times*, 6 September 2008, http://www.nytimes.com/2008/09/07/world/asia/07pstan.html.

24 See the PPP website, http://www.ppp.org.pk/saazcv.html.

25 Personal interviews with Zardari and Sharif, Pakistan, December 2007.

26 'Text of the Charter of Democracy', *Dawn*, 16 May 2006, http://www.dawn.com/2006/05/16/local23.htm.

27 Interviews, New Delhi, December 2007.

28 Ali's *The Duel* offers powerful if sometimes polemical material to suggest that many of Pakistan's current ills are the result of its past relationships with other countries, especially the US.

29 Account given to the author by a senior Pakistani government official, early 2007.

30 Sahar Ahmed, 'Pakistan Won't be Going to IMF: President Zardari', Reuters, 9 September 2008, http://www.reuters.com/article/rbssChemicalsAgricultural/idUSL948890320080909?sp=true.

31 Jane Perlez, 'Rebuffed by China, Pakistan May Seek IMF Aid', *New York Times*, 18 October 2008, http://www.nytimes.com/2008/10/19/world/asia/19zardari.html?ref=asia.

32 'Saudi Response "Positive" to Pakistan's Requests: Tarin', *Dawn*, 5 November 2008, http://www.dawn.com/2008/11/06/top3.htm.

33 'Pakistan Gets $7.6 Billion Loan from IMF', *IMF Survey Magazine* online, 24 November 2008, http://www.imf.org/external/pubs/ft/survey/so/2008/CAR112408C.htm.

34 IMF, 'IMF Executive Board Approves US$7.6 Billion Stand-By Arrangement for Pakistan', press release, 24 November 2008, http://www.imf.org/external/np/sec/pr/2008/pr08303.htm; World Bank, 'Pakistan: Country Overview', available at http://www.worldbank.org.

35 Syed Irfan Raza, 'BISP to be Launched for Fata Women', *Dawn*, http://www.dawn.com/2009/01/05/top8.htm; 'Benazir Income Support Programme from Sep: ECC', *The News*, 31 July 2008, http://www.thenews.com.pk/daily_detail.asp?id=127291.

36 There is increasingly authoritative literature in this area. See in particular Joshua T. White, *Pakistan's Islamist*

Frontier: Islamic Politics and US Policy in Pakistan's North-West Frontier, Center on Faith and International Affairs, Religion and Security Monograph Series, no. 1, 2008; and International Crisis Group, 'Pakistan: The Militant Jihadi Challenge', Asia Report no. 164, 13 March 2009.

37 Matthias Gebauer, 'In the Realm of Mullah Fazlullah', Spiegel Online International, 22 November 2007, http://www.spiegel.de/international/world/0,1518,518962,00.html.

38 See in particular White, *Pakistan's Islamist Frontier*, pp. 89–90.

39 'Official Confirms US Using Pakistani Base to Launch Attacks', FOXNews.com, 19 February 2009, http://www.foxnews.com/politics/elections/2009/02/19/google-image-shows-base-pakistan/.

40 Bill Roggio, 'US Strikes in Pakistan Aimed at Stopping the Next Sept. 11 Attack', *Long War Journal*, 19 September 2008, http://www.longwarjournal.org/archives/2008/09/us_strikes_in_pakist.php.

41 Raja Asghar, 'Outraged Parliament Wants Border Raids Repulsed', *Dawn*, 5 September 2008, http://www.dawn.com/2008/09/05/top1.htm; on the attack itself, see also Roggio, 'Pakistanis Claim US Helicopter-Borne Forces Assaulted Village in South Waziristan', *Long War Journal*, 3 September 2008, http://www.longwarjournal.org/archives/2008/09/pakistanis_claim_us.php.

42 Bobby Ghosh and Mark Thompson, 'The CIA's Silent War in Pakistan', *Time Magazine*, 1 June 2009.

43 Amir Mir, '60 Drone Hits Kill 14 al-Qaeda Men, 687 Civilians', *The News*, international edition, 10 April 2009, http://www.thenews.com.pk/top_story_detail.asp?Id=21440.

44 David Kilcullen and Andrew MacDonald Exum, 'Death from Above, Outrage Down Below', *New York Times*, 16 May 2009, http://www.nytimes.com/2009/05/17/opinion/17exum.html?_r=2&pagewanted=1&ref=opinion.

45 Daniel Markey, 'Hotbed of Terror', Council on Foreign Relations op-ed, 11 August 2008, http://www.cfr.org/publication/16929/hotbed_of_terror.html.

46 Lieutenant-General Tariq Majid, 'Counter-terrorism and Counter-insurgency Efforts by Pakistan: Progress and Prospects', paper presented to the 7th IISS Shangri-La Dialogue, Singapore, 31 May 2008, p. 3.

47 Eric Thompson and Patricio Asfura-Heim, 'Assessments of the Impact of 1206-Funded Projects in Selected Countries', CNA Corporation Center for Strategic Studies, July 2008, p. 23.

48 'Malakand division' is, strictly speaking, an obsolete term denoting a large portion of NWFP that includes the districts of Swat, Chitral, Malakand and others. The term remains in common usage and is used here in recognition of this common currency.

49 Pakistan Defence Secretary Lieutenant-General (Retd) Athar Ali Syed, 'Winning Counter-Insurgency Campaigns: the Pakistan Perspective', presentation to the 8th IISS Shangri-La Dialogue, Singapore, 31 May 2009.

50 'Number of Displaced Persons Exceeds 3 Million: Minister', *Dawn*, 30 May 2009.

51 UN Office for the Coordination of Humanitarian Affairs, 'Pakistan: NWFP Displacement', Situation Report no. 6, 26 June 2009.

52 Thom Shanker and David E. Sanger, 'Pakistan Is Rapidly Adding Nuclear

Arms, U.S. Says', *New York Times*, 18 May 2009.

53 See for example Hilary Synnott, *The Causes and Consequences of South Asia's Nuclear Tests*, Adelphi Paper 332 (Oxford: Oxford University Press for the IISS, 1999), pp 70–4.

54 David E. Sanger, 'Obama's Worst Pakistan Nightmare', *New York Times*, 8 January 2009, http:// www.nytimes.com/2009/01/11/magazine/11pakistan-t.html.

55 'Mullen Believes Pakistan Nukes Secure', Associated Press, 4 May 2009, http://www.military.com/news/article/mullen-believes-pakistan-nukes-secure.html.

56 IISS, *Nuclear Black Markets: Pakistan, A.Q. Khan and the rise of proliferation networks: A net assessment* (London: IISS, 2005).

Chapter Three

1 These regions, which are not marked on most maps, are situated within districts of NWFP. Full details on what they comprise may be found in Naveed Ahmad Shinwari, 'Understanding FATA', Community Appraisal and Motivation Programme, 2008, http://www.understandingfata.org/report%20pdf.html, p. 14.

2 For a fuller explanation of the administration of the tribal regions, see White, *Pakistan's Islamist Frontier: Islamic Politics and US Policy in Pakistan's North-West Frontier*, pp. 15–16.

3 See for example the Government of Balochistan in Exile, 'An Exposé: the Durand Line Agreement is Illegal', 12 May 2006, http://governmentofbalochistan.blogspot.com/2006/05/expose-durand-line-agreement-is.html.

4 Rashid, *Descent into Chaos* (London: Allen Lane, 2008), p. 267.

5 Lieutenant Colonel Sir Ralph Griffith, 'The Frontier Policy of the Government of India', *Journal of the Royal United Services Institution*, February–November 1938, reproduced on pp. 19–36 of the report of a 'Seminar on the Federally Administered Tribal Areas of Pakistan, December 7–8, 2004', Islamabad, organised jointly by the Area Study Centre, University of Peshawar, and the Hanns Seidel Foundation.

6 Louis Dupree, *Afghanistan* (Princeton, NJ: Princeton University Press, 1980), p. 487.

7 Talbot, *Pakistan: A Modern History*, p. 86. 'Pashtunistan' is the name that tends to be used by outsiders for the notion of a Pashtun tribal homeland, known to Pashtuns as 'Pashtunwa'.

8 Dupree, *Afghanistan*, p. 489–540.

9 'The Constitution of the Islamic Republic of Pakistan', http://www.pakistani.org/pakistan/constitution/. Article 1 declares that the FATA are part of Pakistan. Article 246 (see below) defines the tribal areas, of which the FATA are a part. Article 247 sets out how the tribal areas should be administered, placing considerable limits on the role of the federal parliament and the federal judiciary, although it also provides for the possibility of some changes of practice. Article 246:

(a) 'Tribal Areas' means the areas in Pakistan which, immediately before the commencing day, were Tribal Areas, and includes:

(i) the Tribal Areas of Baluchistan and the North-West Frontier Province; and

(ii) the former States of Amb, Chitral, Dir and Swat;

(b) 'Provincially Administered Tribal Areas' means

(i) The districts of Chitral, Dir and Swat (which includes Kalam), [the Tribal Area in Kohistan district,] Malakand Protected Area, the Tribal Area adjoining [Mansehra] district and the former State of Amb; and

(ii) Zhob district, Loralai district (excluding Duki Tehsil), Dalbandis Tehsil of Chagai District and Marri and Bugti tribal territories of Sibi district; and

(c) Federally Administered Tribal Areas includes

(i) Tribal Areas adjoining Peshawar district;

(ii) Tribal Areas adjoining Kohat district;

(iii) Tribal Areas adjoining Bannu district;

(iv) Tribal Areas adjoining Dera Ismail Khan district;

(v) Bajaur Agency;

(v) Orakzai Agency;

(vi) Mohmand Agency;

(vii) Khyber Agency;

(viii) Kurram Agency;

(ix) North Waziristan Agency, and

(x) South Waziristan Agency.

[10] Kamran Arif, 'Tribal Areas Today: "Legal Black-Hole" and "Talibanisation in the Tribal Areas of Pakistan"', paper presented to a seminar at the British Institute of International and Comparative Law, London, 21 October 2008. See also Naveed Ahmad Shinwari,

'Understanding FATA', Community Appraisal and Motivation Programme, 2008, http://www.understandingfata.org/report%20pdf.html, p. 12.

[11] Majid, 'Counter-terrorism and Counter-insurgency Efforts by Pakistan: Progress and Prospects'. The 1998 census records a population of 3.176m. 3.5m is a common estimate for the current population. See White, *Pakistan's Islamist Frontier: Islamic Politics and US Policy in Pakistan's North-West Frontier*, p. 15.

[12] Isabel Hilton, 'The Pashtun Code', *The New Yorker*, 3 December 2001, p. 59.

[13] Descendant of the Prophet Muhammad.

[14] Dupree, *Afghanistan*, p. 126.

[15] *Ibid.*, p. 127.

[16] Yousaf and Adkin, *The Bear Trap: Afghanistan's Untold Story*, pp. 31–6, 90.

[17] Griffith, 'The Frontier Policy of the Government of India', p. 23.

[18] Yousaf and Adkin, *The Bear Trap: Afghanistan's Untold Story*, p. 132.

[19] Repeated to the author by a Pashtun in Peshawar in 2001. See also Anatol Lieven, 'Afghan Terrain', Carnegie Web Commentary, 25 October 2001, http://www.carnegieendowment.org/publications/index.cfm?fa=view&id=829.

[20] Khalid Aziz, 'Extending Stability to Pakistani Tribal Areas', Regional Institute of Policy Research and Training, Peshawar, 2008, paper presented to a conference on 'Pakistan's Federally Administered Tribal Areas: Options for a More Coordinated Policy Approach', Wilton Park, 6–8 November 2008, p. 6; Shinwari, 'Understanding FATA', p. 12.

[21] John D. Negroponte, Testimony before the Senate Foreign Relations Committee, 20 May 2008.

22 Sahibzada Saeed, FATA Secretary to the Governor of NWFP, 'Key Challenges and Development Needs of FATA', paper presented to the 'Seminar on the Federally Administered Tribal Areas of Pakistan, December 7–8, 2004' organised jointly by the Area Study Centre, University of Peshawar, and the Hanns Seidel Foundation, p. 187.

23 Ismail Khan, 'Implications of Repealing FCR', *Dawn*, 30 March 2008.

24 Shinwari, 'Understanding FATA', p. 18.

25 Aziz, 'Extending Stability to Pakistani Tribal Areas', p. 7.

26 *Ibid*. A recent example was the 'President's Task Force on Tribal Reform', which submitted its report in April 2006.

27 Private conversations with senior Pakistani officials, Islamabad, December 2007.

28 Saeed, 'Key Challenges and Development Needs of FATA', p. 9.

29 Majid, 'Counter-terrorism and Counter-insurgency Efforts by Pakistan: Progress and Prospects', p. 3.

30 Embassy of Pakistan, Economic Division, 'FATA Development: 2000 to 2015', 1 July 2008, p. 5, http://www.embassyofpakistanusa.org/forms/FATA Development Program 2008.pdf.

31 'Remarks by the President on a New Strategy for Afghanistan and Pakistan', 27 March 2009, http://www.america.gov/st/texttrans-english/2009/March/20090327121221xjsnommiso.1558496.html&distid=ucs.

32 Conversations in Islamabad, December 2007.

33 Shinwari, 'Understanding FATA'.

34 Interviews with Pashtun and non-Pashtun Pakistanis, Pakistan, December 2008.

35 Frédéric Grare, 'Pakistan: The Resurgence of Baluch Nationalism', Carnegie Paper no. 65, January 2006, p. 6.

36 *Ibid*.

37 'President Musharraf Urges Balochis to Resist those Against Development', Pakistani government press release, 3 September 2007, quoted in International Crisis Group, 'Pakistan: The Forgotten Conflict in Balochistan', Asia Briefing no. 69, 22 October 2007.

38 Farhan Bokhari, 'Bugti's Killing will Harm Musharraf', *Gulf News*, 3 September 2006.

39 See for example International Crisis Group, 'Pakistan: The Forgotten Conflict in Balochistan'.

40 'Riots as Baloch Chiefs Found Dead', BBC News, 9 April 2009.

41 Amir Mir, 'Dire Prophecies', *Pakistan Today*, 17 February 2006.

42 Selig S. Harrison, 'Pakistan's Baluch Insurgency', *Le Monde Diplomatique*, October 2006.

43 Grare, 'Pakistan: The Resurgence of Baluch Nationalism'.

44 Mir, 'Dire Prophecies'; Sanaullah Baloch, 'Understanding the Crisis in Balochistan', presentation to the IISS, London, 24 April 2006.

45 'Pakistan Launches Strategic Port', BBC News, 20 March 2007, http://news.bbc.co.uk/1/hi/world/south_asia/6469725.stm.

46 International Crisis Group, 'Pakistan: The Forgotten Conflict in Balochistan'.

Chapter Four

1   Though they did not have political control over the waging or the direction of the war. The Pakistani prime minister decided not to involve British officers in the planning for the war. Nawaz, *Crossed Swords*, p. 48.

2   The following very compressed account draws in particular on Chari, Cheema and Cohen, *Four Crises and a Peace Process*.

3   In seeking to distance the government from its history of inciting terrorism, Musharraf's speech of January 2002 in which he announced bans on Lashkar-e-Tayiba and Jaysh-e-Mohammad (see Chapter 2) effectively admitted that there had been such involvement in the past. Ziring, *Pakistan in the Twentieth Century*, pp. 321–3; Hussain, *Frontline Pakistan*, pp. 107–8.

4   Talbot, *Pakistan: A Modern History*, p. 235.

5   Third parties who have offered unsolicited advice to India on a resolution of the Kashmir issue, such as British Foreign Secretaries Robin Cook in 1997 and David Miliband in January 2009, have been sharply criticised for doing so.

6   Chari, Cheema and Cohen, *Four Crises and a Peace Process*, p. 21.

7   Victoria Schofield, *Kashmir in Conflict* (London: IB Tauris, 2000) pp. 151 and 186.

8   Mark Mazzetti and Salman Masood, 'US Intelligence Focuses on Pakistani Group', *New York Times*, 28 November 2008, http://www.nytimes.com/2008/11/29/world/asia/29intel.html?_r=1;Rashid, *Descent into Chaos*, p. 53.

9   Hussain, *Frontline Pakistan*, p. 35.

10 Jayshree Bajoria, 'India–Afghanistan Relations', Council on Foreign Relations Backgrounder, 23 October 2008, http://www.cfr.org/publication/17474/indiaafghanistan_relations.html; R.K. Gundu and T.C. Schaffer, 'India and Pakistan in Afghanistan: Hostile Sports', CSIS *South Asia Monitor*, no. 117, 3 April 2008, http://csis.org/files/media/csis/pubs/sam117.pdf.

11 Both the Indian proposal and the Pakistani complaint were aired by those countries' representatives at the IISS Shangri-La Dialogue, Singapore, 29–31 May 2009.

12 Anand Gopal, 'Coordinated Kabul Assault Shows Taliban Strength', *Christian Science Monitor*, 12 February 2009, http://www.csmonitor.com/2009/0212/p07s02-woap.html.

13 'Home Ministry Announces Measures to Enhance Security', Government of India Press Information Bureau, press release, 11 December 2007, http://pib.nic.in/release/release.asp?relid=45446.

14 Somini Sengupta, 'Dossier Gives Details of Mumbai Attacks', *New York Times*, 6 January 2008, http://www.nytimes.com/2009/01/07/world/asia/07india.html?_r=2.

15 'Pakistan "Holds 71" over Mumbai', BBC News, 15 January 2008, http://news.bbc.co.uk/1/hi/world/south_asia/7830276.stm.

16 Nawaz, *Crossed Swords*, p. 548.

17 Ashley J. Tellis, 'Mumbai Attacks: Implications for the US', Testimony to the Senate Committee on Homeland Security and Governmental Affairs, 28 January 2009, http://www.carnegieendowment.org/publications/index.cfm?fa=view&id=22676&prog=zgp&proj=zsa.

18 *Ibid.*

[19] Hussain, *Frontline Pakistan*, p. 115–16.

[20] Masood Haider and Anwar Iqbal, 'Pakistan, India to Make Fresh Start on Kashmir', *Dawn*, 25 September 2004, http://www.dawn.com/2004/09/25/top5.htm.

[21] Syed Rifaat Hussain, 'Pakistan's Changing Outlook on Kashmir', *Kashmir Affairs*, March 2008, http://www.kashmiraffairs.org/rifaat_hussain_pak_change_outlook_kashmir.html.

[22] 'India–Pakistan Composite Dialogue Stalled', *Economic Times*, 16 December 2008, http://economictimes.indiatimes.com/India-Pakistan_composite_dialogue_stalled/articleshow/3847316.cms.

[23] And many commentators: see for example Coll, 'The Back Channel', *The New Yorker*, 2 March 2009.

[24] Private discussions, New Delhi, December 2007.

[25] Private discussion, Islamabad, December 2007.

[26] 'The Future of Kashmir', BBC News, http://news.bbc.co.uk/1/shared/spl/hi/south_asia/03/kashmir_future/html/default.stm.

[27] Musharraf, *In the Line of Fire*, p. 56.

[28] Yousaf and Adkin, *The Bear Trap*, p. 84. The authors are careful to emphasise that nothing more than mules was supplied along the route, saying that 'not one bullet' came down the highway.

[29] For a brief account of the disputes between China and India, see Synnott, *The Causes and Consequences of South Asia's Nuclear Tests*.

[30] Talbot, *Pakistan: A Modern History*, p. 224.

[31] Gareth Jennings, 'JF-17 Production Commences', *Jane's*, 24 January 2008, http://www.janes.com/news/defence/air/jdw/jdw080124_2_n.shtml.

[32] George Perkovich, *India's Nuclear Bomb* (Berkeley, CA: University of California Press, 1999), p. 196.

[33] Robert Shuey and Shirley Kan, 'China Missile and Nuclear Proliferation', Congressional Research Service Issue Brief, 29 September 1995.

[34] Synnott, *The Causes and Consequences of South Asia's Nuclear Tests*, pp. 15–16. See also Perkovich, *India's Nuclear Bomb*.

[35] Bennett-Jones, *Pakistan: Eye of the Storm*, pp. 205–6.

[36] 'New Openings for Increasing Trade with China', *PakTribune*, 17 August 2007, http://www.paktribune.com/business/newsdetail.php?nid=4327.

[37] Pakistan Finance Ministry, 'Economic Survey 2006–7: Overview of the Economy', http://www.finance.gov.pk/admin/images/survey/chapters/overview_06_07.pdf.

[38] 'Joint Statement Between China and Pakistan, October 2008', 16 October 2008, http://www.cfr.org/publication/17543/joint_statement_between_china_and_pakistan_october_2008.html.

[39] Perlez, 'Monetary Fund Approves $7.5bn Loan to Pakistan', *New York Times*, 25 November 2008, http://www.nytimes.com/2008/11/26/world/asia/26pstan.html?scp=1&sq=china loan to pakistan&st=cse.

[40] Talal Malik, 'India–Pakistan Trade with Gulf Hits $36bn', ArabianBusiness.com, 14 August 2007, http://www.arabianbusiness.com/497795-india-pakistan-trade-with-gcc-hits-36bn.

[41] For much of the information in this section, see Bruce Riedel, 'Saudi Arabia: Nervously Watching Pakistan', Brookings, 28 January 2008, http://www.brookings.edu/opinions/2008/0128_saudi_arabia_riedel.aspx. See also Arnaud de Borchgrave, 'Pakistan,

Saudi Arabia in Secret Nuke Pact', *Washington Times*, 22 October 2003.

[42] Nawaz, *Crossed Swords*, p. 372; Coll, *Ghost Wars*, pp. 73, 81, 296–7.

[43] 'Weapons of Mass Destruction: Saudi Arabia Special Weapons', Global Security.org, http://www. globalsecurity.org/wmd/world/ saudi/.

[44] IISS, *Nuclear Programmes in the Middle East: In the shadow of Iran* (London: IISS, 2008).

[45] Riedel, 'Saudi Arabia: Nervously Watching Pakistan'.

Conclusion

[1] Such language has reportedly been used by Chairman of US Joint Chiefs of Staff Committee Admiral Mike Mullen. Hussain, 'Many Reported Dead as Pakistan Army Attacks Taleban Near Swat', The Times, 27 April 2009.

[2] 'The Constitution of Pakistan: Annex: The Objectives Resolution', http://www.pakistani.org/pakistan/ constitution/annex_objres.html/.

[3] 'Assistant Secretary Boucher: "President Musharraf's Goals for Pakistan Compatible with US Objectives"', US embassy in Islamabad press release, 24 April 2006, http://islamabad.usembassy. gov/pakistan/h06042402.html.

[4] 'Remarks by the President on a New Strategy for Afghanistan and Pakistan'.

[5] See for example HM Government, 'UK Policy in Afghanistan and Pakistan: The Way Forward', April 2009, p. 13, http://www.dfid.gov.uk/Documents/ publications/Cross-government/ ukgov_afghanistan_pakistan.pdf.

[6] Of the $11.2bn total direct overt US aid and military disbursements to Pakistan between 2002 and 2008, $8.1bn was security-related, $2.4bn was debt relief and 'budget support' cash transfers, and only $677m went on development assistance, welfare and food aid. 'Direct Overt US Aid and Military Reimbursements to Pakistan, FY2002–FY2009', prepared for the Congressional Research Service by K. Alan Kronstadt, specialist in South Asian affairs, 16 October 2008, http:// pdf.usaid.gov/pdf_docs/PCAAB883. pdf.

[7] 'Remarks by the President on a New Strategy for Afghanistan and Pakistan'.

[8] See for example 'Pakistan Opinion Poll Indicates Sharp Turn Against Taliban', VOA News, 1 July 2009, http://www. voanews.com/bangla/2009-07-01-voa5. cfm; and the International Republican Institute, 'IRI Index: Pakistan', opinion poll, 12 December 2007, http://www. iri.org/mena/pakistan/pdfs/2007-12- 12-pakistan-poll-index.pdf.

[9] The BBC suggested in 2008 that nearly 75% of NATO's supplies to Afghanistan travelled through Pakistan. Damian Grammaticas, 'Pakistan's Spreading Taleban War', BBC News, 26 November 2008, http://news.bbc.co.uk/1/hi/world/ south_asia/7750542.stm.

[10] See for example Seth Jones, 'Pakistan's Dangerous Game', *Survival*, vol. 49, no. 1, Spring 2007, p. 15. Other observers seem to have given up on the utility

11 of external help of any kind: John R. Schmidt, 'The Unravelling of Pakistan', *Survival*, vol. 51, no. 3, June–July 2009, p. 51.

11 Tellis, 'Pakistan and the War on Terror: Conflicted Goals, Compromised Performance', Carnegie Endowment Report, 2008, p. 39; for Obama's statement to this effect, see Dan Balz, 'Obama Says He Would Take Fight to Pakistan', *Washington Post*, 2 August 2007.

12 An American commentator used this term at a conference on 'The Impact of Western Strategy on Muslim South Asia', Royal United Services Institute, 3 December 2007.

13 For an example of such arguments, see Jones, 'Pakistan's Dangerous Game', p. 28.

14 The Defence Committee of the Cabinet is traditionally Pakistan's main mechanism for civilian–military consultation and decision-making on strategic and politico-military affairs. In 2001, Musharraf set up the National Security Council in addition, with a remit to perform broadly the same task. The new body very seldom met. In February 2009, Prime Minister Gilani promised to abolish the National Security Council and use instead a restructured version of the Defence Committee. It is unclear whether the council has in fact been abolished, but in any event, neither body is much used, to the extent that both are essentially moribund.

15 It was thus surprising to see a senior NATO figure in early 2009 officially promoting the idea of changing the constitutional status of the FATA, at a time when the concept is deeply controversial within Pakistan: Karl-Heinz Lather, 'NATO in Afghanistan and Better Cooperation with Afghanistan', World Security Network, 19 February 2009, http://www.worldsecuritynetwork.com/showArticle3.cfm?Article_ID=17193.

16 The EU has developed much expertise in international police training and could make a particular contribution in this field. On remuneration, policy analyst and scholar Anatol Lieven, in discussion with the author in June 2009, estimated that it would cost only $25m to double police pay in NWFP.

17 Rashid, *Descent into Chaos*, p. 269.

18 See for example Nasser Yousaf, 'Time for Holbrooke to Play Durand', *Dawn*, 9 June 2009, http://www.dawn.com/wps/wcm/connect/dawn-content-library/dawn/news/pakistan/12-time-for-holbrooke-to-play-durand--bi-01.

19 'Karzai, Musharraf in Terror Vow', BBC News, 30 April 2007, http://news.bbc.co.uk/1/hi/world/south_asia/6607743.stm; Pak–Afghan Border Needs a Fence like US–Mexico: Gilani', *The News*, 4 July 2009, http://www.thenews.com.pk/top_story_detail.asp?Id=23082.

20 For a range of views on this issue – most in favour of making some kind of approach under certain conditions – see Council on Foreign Relations, 'Six Experts on Negotiating with the Taliban', 20 March 2009, http://www.cfr.org/publication/18893/six_experts_on_negotiating_with_the_taliban.html. In July 2009, British Foreign Secretary David Miliband belatedly took on the sceptics and advocated drawing insurgents into domestic political processes. Miliband, 'NATO's Mission in Afghanistan: The Political Strategy', speech at NATO Headquarters, Brussels, 27 July 2009.

21 See 'EU Must Bring its Expertise to Pakistan', Atlantic-Community.org,

18 June 2009, http://www.atlantic-community.org/index/articles/view/EU_Must_Bring_Its_Expertise_to_Pakistan.

22 'Donors Pledge $5bn Aid for Pakistan', CNN, 17 April 2009, http://edition.cnn.com/2009/WORLD/asiapcf/04/17/pakistan.tokyo.aid/index.html; Council of the European Union, 'EU–Pakistan Summit: Joint Statement', 17 June 2009, http://www.consilium.europa.eu/uedocs/cms_Data/docs/pressdata/en/declarations/108562.pdf.

23 Christina Lamb quoting Amir Sultan Tarar, a 'Pakistani intelligence agent who trained Mullah Omar', in 'The Taliban Will Never be Defeated', *Sunday Times*, 7 June 2009.

Adelphi books are published eight times a year by Routledge Journals, an imprint of Taylor & Francis, 4 Park Square, Milton Park, Abingdon, Oxfordshire OX14 4RN, UK.

A subscription to the institution print edition, ISSN 0567-932X, includes free access for any number of concurrent users across a local area network to the online edition, ISSN 1478-5145.

2009 Annual Adelphi Subscription Rates		
Institution	£381	$669 USD
Individual	£222	$378 USD
Online only	£361	$636 USD

Dollar rates apply to subscribers in all countries except the UK and the Republic of Ireland where the pound sterling price applies. All subscriptions are payable in advance and all rates include postage. Journals are sent by air to the USA, Canada, Mexico, India, Japan and Australasia. Subscriptions are entered on an annual basis, i.e. January to December. Payment may be made by sterling cheque, dollar cheque, international money order, National Giro, or credit card (Amex, Visa, Mastercard).

For more information, visit our website: **http://www.informaworld.com/adelphipapers.**

For a complete and up-to-date guide to Taylor & Francis journals and books publishing programmes, and details of advertising in our journals, visit our website: **http://www.informaworld.com.**

Ordering information:
USA/Canada: Taylor & Francis Inc., Journals Department, 325 Chestnut Street, 8th Floor, Philadelphia, PA 19106, USA. **UK/Europe/Rest of World:** Routledge Journals, T&F Customer Services, T&F Informa UK Ltd., Sheepen Place, Colchester, Essex, CO3 3LP, UK.

Advertising enquiries to:
USA/Canada: The Advertising Manager, Taylor & Francis Inc., 325 Chestnut Street, 8th Floor, Philadelphia, PA 19106, USA. Tel: +1 (800) 354 1420. Fax: +1 (215) 625 2940.

UK/Europe/Rest of World: The Advertising Manager, Routledge Journals, Taylor & Francis, 4 Park Square, Milton Park, Abingdon, Oxfordshire OX14 4RN, UK. Tel: +44 (0) 20 7017 6000. Fax: +44 (0) 20 7017 6336.

The print edition of this journal is printed on ANSI conforming acid-free paper by Bell & Bain, Glasgow, UK.

1944-5571(2009)49:3;1-M